Praise for *White. Blonde. Jew.*

"Alyssa Rosenheck has written a courageous and timely book. *White. Blonde. Jew.* goes far beyond explanation, offering readers practical insights that invite personal reflection and action. By breaking through stereotypes, Rosenheck reminds us that each one of us has the power to stand up, speak truth, and challenge the false narratives that continue to distort the conversation about Jews and Israel."

—Rabbi Raphael Shore, author, producer, and founder

"*White. Blonde. Jew.* bravely confronts what many have chosen to ignore—the ways modern-day antisemitism has insidiously infiltrated our day-to-day lives. What sets Alyssa's work apart is her willingness to honestly examine difficult topics and conversations that we have either avoided altogether or allowed to separate us for far too long. What makes this book exceptional is its ability to provide solutions for bridging these divides in lasting and meaningful ways. This book is a seminal work for all who are tired of being ostracized for fear of choosing the 'wrong' side. You cannot change what you are unwilling to confront—and *White. Blonde. Jew.* is a blueprint for both."

—Sandra Hagee Parker, chairwoman of CUFI Action Fund

"A bold and unflinching book that takes on antisemitism, misinformation, and the weaponization of race. Rosenheck's call to 'reclaim center' is as timely as it is necessary—and her personal stories make it impossible to look away."

—Fleur Hassan Nahoum, Israel foreign ministry special envoy for trade and innovation

"*White. Blonde. Jew.* is a fearless and deeply human dismantling of the labels meant to silence us. With unflinching clarity and lived experience, Alyssa Rosenheck exposes how extremism, antisemitism, and identity politics distort truth and offers a courageous blueprint for reclaiming moral center. This book challenges, steadies, heals, and ultimately reminds us what integrity looks like in a world addicted to outrage."

—Dr. Sheila Nazarian, plastic surgeon, TV personality, and activist

"In her newest book, *White. Blonde. Jew.*, award-winning photographer and author Alyssa Rosenheck is as direct as the title her book bears. Deeply revealing and insightful, Alyssa takes her reader on a raw journey, professionally and personally, sharing both the best and worst of humanity. Despite being immersed in the world of "the arts"—where artists tout their tolerance—Alyssa experienced everything but acceptance. And, when she dared to speak up and be heard, she was further marginalized, ostracized, and censored. Maligned for being white, blonde, and Jewish, Rosenheck nevertheless fearlessly lays out uncensored, timeless truths, not only to her benefit, but for ours, as well. Sharing her story, while weaving in history from the time of Moses through post the October 7 massacre, Alyssa succinctly journeys through the history of the Jewish people. Through her lens, she brings into focus these ancient people, whose tale of survival despite innumerable persecutions is marked by resilience, inextinguishable joy, and pride in their faith. And in near parallel, she also outlines the history of the insidious hatred that seeks to destroy this faith, laying bare the many guises of antisemitism, racism, and prejudice. Alyssa illustrates the endless, iterative battle between good and evil, and the strength it takes to stand for what is right. Her bold voice and fortitude in the face of prejudice inherent to the DEI movement make clear that timidity, assimilation, and acquiescence only serve to lend might to hate. It is only through speaking out with moral clarity that this iniquity can be defeated. Alyssa's words serve as an inspiration to us all. As she dared herself in a way most do not, she empowers and challenges her readers to live up to their full potential for the imperative of good."

—Julie Strauss Levin, senior counsel at America First Legal Foundation, and Mark Levin, nationally syndicated talk radio host, Fox News analyst, and #1 *New York Times* bestselling author

"Alyssa Rosenheck's *White. Blond. Jew.* is a raw, emotional, and critical exploration of modern antisemitism, weaving her personal, life-altering experiences with crucial historical context. She offers an essential look at the contemporary Jewish experience, particularly in the wake of October 7, a watershed moment for global Jewry. More than just a memoir, this book provides incredible opportunities for dialogue with suggested thought exercises for book clubs. It's a fantastic and important read for anyone who has ever felt marginalized or misunderstood, or wishes to gain a deeper understanding of the challenges facing the Jewish community today. This is a powerful call to truth, understanding, and action, and a reminder to stand strong and proud even during the most challenging times."

—Julie Paris, Mid-Atlantic regional director of StandWithUs

"In 1974, Aleksander Solzhenitsyn insisted that Soviet totalitarianism existed not just because of the lies and repression of the government, but because of the passive participation of the public, because of their unwillingness to tell the difficult and dangerous truth. Above all else, Rosenheck's *White. Blonde. Jew.* does just that—in confronting hatred, in battling ignorance, and in revealing her vulnerability in the face of it all."

—Rankin Sherling, PhD, associate director of the Declaration of Independence Center for the Study of American Freedom at the University of Mississippi

WHITE.
BLONDE.
JEW.

Also by Alyssa Rosenheck

The New Southern Style: The Interiors of a Lifestyle and Design Movement

WHITE. BLONDE. JEW.

A Call to End Extremism, Speak Up, and Reclaim Center

ALYSSA ROSENHECK

BENBELLA

BenBella Books, Inc.
Dallas, TX

BenBella

BenBella Books, Inc.
8080 N. Central Expressway
Suite 1400
Dallas, TX 75206
benbellabooks.com
Send feedback to feedback@benbellabooks.com

Printed in the United States of America
10 9 8 7 6 5 4 3 2 1

Library of Congress Control Number: 2026014519
ISBN 9781637748329 (hardcover)
ISBN 9781637748336 (electronic)

Editing by Rick Chillot
Copyediting by Elizabeth Degenhard
Proofreading by Jenny Bridges and Jill Kramer
Indexing by WordCo Indexing Services
Text design and composition by PerfecType, Nashville, TN
Art direction by Alyssa Rosenheck
Cover photography by Nate Griffin
Printed by Lake Book Manufacturing

For those stolen too early,
Your light outlives the darkness.

CONTENTS

A LETTER TO YOU

Before we begin, I just want to say: thank you.

Thank you for being here, for picking up this book, for being open to this conversation. Whatever brought you to these pages, I hope you find something that resonates, challenges, and strengthens you.

This book is divided into three sections, but at its core, it's about something we all share: the search for truth, the courage to speak up, and the need to push past the divisions that try to keep us apart.

No matter your background, faith, or beliefs, this journey is for you. Because the struggles we face today don't belong to just one group. They affect us all.

White. Blonde. Jew. isn't just about Jewish identity. It's about how we navigate a fractured world, how we hold on to what's right when the noise around us tries to distort it, and how we build bridges instead of walls. This isn't a matter of accumulating knowledge. It calls for truth and transformation. This book is yours to navigate. You can read it cover to cover, following the journey as it unfolds, or you can jump around, picking the chapters that call to you first, choosing your own adventure along the way.

At the end of each chapter, you'll find reflections and book club activities, tools designed to help you process, discuss, and live these ideas. I created the P.A.C.E. method—Pause, Analyze, Contemplate, Engage, because in a world that moves too fast, we need to slow down, think deeply, and choose how we respond. We need to P.A.C.E. ourselves. Whether you're reading these pages alone or with a group, these moments of reflection are here to challenge assumptions, deepen conversations, and help us grow, together.

So take what you need from the chapters ahead. Question, wrestle with the ideas, and bring them into your world. Because when we commit to this kind of honest engagement, we're not just learning. We're shaping a future built on truth, courage, and compassion.

WHITE. BLONDE. JEW.

Why would a photographer—someone who has spent years capturing beauty—step so far outside the comfort of her own genre to create a book like this one? The truth is, I had no choice. When I watched my community's voice being erased, and history being rewritten in real time, standing on the sidelines was never an option. It's not how I was raised. For better or for worse, I will always use my voice and my resources to correct the very ideologies that have been so pervasive throughout history seeking to cause more harm than good. I know that others feel the same. Fighting hate has never been a solo act; in fact, it's a team sport.

For me, writing this book was an act of defiance. A refusal. A deeply personal way of saying *no*, and a middle finger to publishing companies for ostracizing Jews. *No* to dangerous ideas that have crept into the mainstream. *No* to the complicity of silence. And *no* to staying stagnant when everything in me demanded growth.

Although our paths may look different, I want my writing to highlight that shared emotional core that connects us. I hope you see yourself in these pages. These words are here to hold your hand—to challenge, to heal, to push, and, most importantly, to bring us back to a shared collective center.

Full disclosure: writing this book was a risk. To my career, to my personal safety, to cleansing my social circle. A risk I took willingly, but not without hesitation.

I also wrote this book as a promise—to myself and to those of us standing on the rooftop of the Hostage Forum in Tel Aviv on a cool February afternoon in 2024. That moment, that circle, was more than a gathering. It was a declaration.

I was on this trip because of my lens, my words, and the unwavering bond of friendship with a woman I will forever be grateful for.

My close friend Alex and I had been searching for the right way to get to Israel after the war began, and when this opportunity came, we knew—we felt—we sensed—we had to be there. What unfolded over the next four days would change us both.

More than twenty meetings followed, back-to-back, each one a reckoning with history, loss, and resilience. And then, near the trip's end, Christine (another dear friend), Alex, and I found ourselves in a circle of over thirty human beings, each of us asked to speak our takeaways out loud.

I chose to go last.

The air was thick with something indescribable: grief, pride, and resolve woven together, voices carrying a hymn of resilience. Alex, seated to my right, spoke early on. She and her husband had moved from Israel, yet she shared how, in the early days of building her start-up, she made a promise to designate a headquarters there, to contribute to the economy and ensure a lasting connection to the community. That commitment has since shaped her company's growth in ways she never could have imagined. I couldn't be prouder.

More voices followed, each sharing what they had seen, the survivors they had met, the impact this trip had left on their souls.

Then came Christine. She spoke with a fire in her voice, more determined than ever to return to the States and make a difference. And she has, becoming a force on the East Coast, bringing in speakers from across the world (myself included) to share the truth with her community.

Then, it was my turn.

I stood before Ivy League business professors, tech entrepreneurs, and industry leaders—but in that moment, titles dissolved. We weren't just professionals or visitors. I shared how we were witnesses. We were sons and daughters of the land, connected not just by history, but by something deeper. By responsibility, by love, by the unshakable truth that Israel is more than a place on a map. It is home. A home we may not all live in physically, but one we are bound to protect with everything we have.

That day, I made a promise. G-d willing, if I were given the opportunity to write another book, I would dedicate it to the lives that were taken from us too soon. I would pour every word, every truth, every unrelenting fight onto the page—not just to remember, but to refuse erasure. To refuse silence. Because when our collective home is at stake, not using our voice is not just a failure: It is a betrayal.

A QUICK NOTE ON WHY G-D IS MISSING AN "O"

"Please don't tell me that writing the Lord's name is disrespectful now too! What is this world coming to when everyone is so offended?"

She came in hot. It was late in the evening, and I was drained from the day—but not enough to ignore my human side. I've always believed in leading with kindness, especially when something holds deep value to me. Plus, she had a point. We are living in a world where people seem to be constantly suiting up for battle, ready to pounce on their keyboards at the slightest provocation. Ironically, she was annoyed by the very phenomenon she was exemplifying.

She responded to an Instagram story I had shared about the hostages—an emotional post followed by a mindful note and a prayer I wrote. But what caught her attention? My choice to write "G-d" instead of spelling it out in full.

I could feel her energy through the screen, the frustration woven into her words. Something told me she'd had a rough day, so I decided to soften the moment, to meet her with understanding instead of defensiveness.

There are things you grow up with that simply stick, and for me, one of those things is leaving out the "o" in "G-d." It's a sign of reverence in Judaism. A way of acknowledging the sanctity of the divine name and preventing it from being casually discarded or erased. It's about preservation, a small but meaningful tradition that connects me to generations before me.

In a culture where values and symbols are rapidly diminishing, I believe it's important to hold on to the ones that ground us.

Of course, if you ask three Jews how they write the name, you'll probably get three different answers. And that's the beauty of it—our faith is both deeply personal and endlessly diverse.

PROMISES

This book is that promise fulfilled. A testament that even as the world shifts beneath our feet, even as narratives are rewritten and truths are twisted, the voices of those we lost and who continue to physically fight will not be forgotten.

The stories, the presence, the humanity of those murdered on October 7th . . . they are not just memories. They are a fire carried forward. A flame of hope, a declaration of light, a defiance against those who would see us disappear.

Finally, I just want to say thank you—again. The fact that this book is in your hands right now means something. It's a reflection of your curiosity, your willingness to explore beyond the familiar, and a quiet but powerful act of engagement in a time when so many choose to look away. It means you're here, open, and ready to wrestle with things that may challenge you. That alone matters more than I can say.

And so, we write. We create. We remember. And we fight together.

WHY THIS TITLE? WHY THIS STRUCTURE?

Let's talk about this book's title: *White. Blonde. Jew.*

I've never subscribed to identity politics. I believe in character. In how a person shows up in the world. In integrity, not surface-level labels. I believe who we are is revealed in our actions, not our appearance.

But the reality is: these three words—white, blonde, Jew—are often the first things people see.

Until I open my mouth.

Some people are going to criticize the title. I already know that. But here's the truth: the joke's on them. They gave me this title. These were the words used to box me in, shut me down, or make me feel like I didn't belong.

So I took them, and I made them mine.

I turned the slurs, the stereotypes, and the assumptions into structure. I turned the projection into education. I alchemized hate into a unifying book.

Each section in the book, "White," "Blonde," and "Jew," is a chapter in how the world has tried to quiet us. They're also the categories I've had to examine, question, and ultimately dismantle in order to reclaim my sanity—and my courage.

But let me tell you what these sections *really* are.

The White section isn't just about how I've been reduced or shamed for something I didn't choose. It's about what happens when conversations about privilege, whiteness, oppression, and geopolitics get weaponized. When DEI becomes dogma. When schools start teaching ideology instead of inquiry. This part of the book is a wake-up call—and a guide. It will help you recognize the dangerous groupthink creeping into your community, and give you tools to start using your voice in the local spaces that matter most.

The Blonde section is, yes, about what people see before they hear me—but it's also the soft center of the book. The heartbeat. This is where I explore the roots (Get it? Ha! Not a natural blonde, so roots for days) of stereotype, softness, and strength. I challenge the misinformation and disinformation that shape so much of our culture—and reimagine what it means to own our appearance without being owned by it. In a world obsessed with optics, this chapter brings us back to something we all share.

The final section—Jew—is the one that cuts deepest. Here I go beyond headlines and hashtags to share what it means to *live* through them. It's about what's been erased, rewritten, or twisted—and what we have to recover to stay human. I tell personal stories. I walk through history. I reckon with grief, rage, and memory. And I offer a path forward, grounded in truth, that will sharpen your critical thinking and strengthen your humanity.

These aren't just three labels. They're three *openings*.

And by the end of this book, I hope you'll see yourself—your courage, your questions, your voice—more clearly in each of them.

This book is what happens *after* I speak. It's what happens when a human being refuses to be summed up in a glance, and decides to tell the whole damn story.

So if the title makes people uncomfortable, great.

It's supposed to.

If it makes you curious, even better.

Because this isn't just about labels—it's about *breaking* them. It's about remembering that we are just a small link in a greater chain. It's about our responsibility to one another.

This is not a book about identity politics.

It's a book about what matters when all of that gets stripped away: character, truth, and the courage to speak anyway.

This is where we begin.

Now watch what I do with it—and I hope it inspires you to do the same.

WHITE.

BLONDE.

JEW.

CHAPTER 1
PRIVILEGE IS SAFETY

> I woke up soaked in sweat, my tee plastered to my skin. A nightmare had shaken me from sleep—but the real horror had already happened. It was all over our screens.
>
> I reached for my phone in the dark and typed into the Notes app, barely breathing:
>
> If my light skin equals "privilege," then why didn't it keep some of my brothers and sisters safe?
>
> **—Alyssa Rosenheck, 10.8.2023**

I spent the first decade of my career chasing light, literally. I documented how it moves through our most intimate spaces, our homes. I studied its rise and fall, the way it dances with shadows, revealing its depth and range.

In many ways, I built my career around light, using it as a mirror to reflect our humanity, our goodness. But now, as the world has shifted, so has my lens. This is the season where I balance the scales, not just by seeking the light, but also by confronting the shadows that have grown far too large in our society, shadows I can no longer unsee.

On October 7th, 2023, from the safety of my home in America, I watched in disbelief as evil acts were recorded and distributed in real time.

I allowed myself just one day to weep, overwhelmed by the calculated barbarism, amplified by amphetamines, that led to the second-largest massacre of Jewish lives since the Holocaust.[1] It was a cruelty so unfathomable.

I am not naïve to the existence of hate and ignorance in this world; they are undeniable truths. Yet the magnitude of evil unleashed that day upon innocent children, women, young girls, men, and the elderly should be universally intolerable. The brutality I witnessed left me enraged, sleepless, haunted by visions of rape, and restless as the world remained silent.

Pelvises shattered. Nails driven into the most sacred parts of the body. Gunshots ripped through wombs that will no longer yield life. Breasts cut off, totally severed,[2] then tossed aside like scraps for dogs.[3]

The value of life lies in the respect we show for the dead, even lives stolen by those who have no reverence for the living.

Survivors of October 7th recall the bloodcurdling screams of women as their bodies were violated and entered without consent. Their cries of resistance echoed until they were silenced by execution or decapitation.

The perpetrators did not carry out these heinous acts in the shadows. Gazan terrorists and "journalists" documented the atrocities, glorifying their savagery as if the victims were nothing more than prey in a cruel and calculated hunt. Their celebration of death, captured in vivid detail, reduced human lives to trophies of their twisted triumph.

These were not solely acts of murder against innocents; they were calculated spectacles meant to horrify, to spread the currency of fear.

The West cannot wash its hands of the blood.

The terrorists' videos and photos found their way into prestigious Western platforms like *The New York Times*, the Associated Press, and *TIME*.[4] The media's aim was not to expose the barbarity, but to tell the perpetrators' narrative. The Reynolds Journalism Institute at the University of Missouri, the most revered journalism school in the United States, even granted awards for the despicable images.[5]

I was haunted by the images and trapped in a cycle of nightmares. I was not alone. Trauma lingers, even in the silence, even in the moments we cannot speak. When your people are strategically hunted, their suffering is a mark on your soul. Even now, as I write these words, tears burn my eyes. These words are a release, yet they do not even begin to capture the weight of that silence or what's at stake.

One photo in particular shook me to my core.

The one behind the lens tells the story.

The story they have access to.

The story they prepared for.

As a photographer, I know all too well how the person behind the lens crafts the story—two things were evident to me in the photo: The photographers had access to the terrorists, and they were prepared for the shoot.

I studied the image of twenty-two-year-old victim Shani Louk.[6] She lay face down in the bed of a white truck. Four men loomed over her, their legs pinning her lifeless body in place, preventing her from rolling off the bed of the truck. It was as if she was prey they had hunted, and were taking her back to further sacrifice her lifeless body as they celebrated. Her leg hung off the edge of the open bed of the truck, her limbs contorted, bloodied and broken, her breast half exposed.

The men were heavily armed; one wore Nike apparel with the slogan "Just Do It." And they did. They destroyed, they tortured, and they were champions.

If you study an image long enough, it reveals far more than just the subjects within the frame. It tells a story about the one composing it, their perspective, their relationship to the subject, and the truths they decide to expose or obscure. In every shot, there is a subtle imprint of the photographer's worldview, a message woven into the frame, even if it's unspoken.

The Associated Press credited Hassan Eslaiah, Yousef Masoud, Ali Mahmud, and Hatem Ali in their heinous photo series. All four freelance photographers were based in Gaza.[7] But it was Ali Mahmud whose lens captured Shani Louk.

I looked at the photo and wondered: Why was he spared from the massacre? Why was he granted immunity from distributing photos of international acts of terror? If neutrality was his aim, why did he continue pressing the shutter instead of alerting the authorities?

The faces of the men in the truck are triumphant and friendly—fueled with adrenaline and victory. I didn't want to study such a horrible photo, but I could not unsee the truth: the proximity to this act of terror cannot be chalked up to "great timing." In the first moments of a war, after rockets rained down on Israel, this photographer was welcomed safely to the front lines. It didn't make sense. Hamas did not only kill Jews on October 7th. The lives of many Arabs and Christians were taken on that day. No, this photographer didn't just have a fixer on speed dial; he must have been part of the very cause he was documenting, based off his access and safety.

I shuddered. If true, that means the West is rewarding terrorism. It would be like giving ISIS an award for best short-doc after they livestreamed beheadings. It's completely absurd and incredibly dangerous. This grotesque distortion of truth doesn't only perpetuate a cycle of dehumanization; it erodes the global understanding of humanity's most sacred principle: life and safety.

Before the war, I saw myself as a purpose-driven visual storyteller, an interiors and architectural photographer, and a writer. My first book, *The New Southern Style*, was published in 2020. The objective behind my book was to incorporate an element of substance and diversity into an industry that only celebrates style. I'm one of the very few Jewish voices in the South who's been educating communities about antisemitism since that point.

My work demonstrates how creativity humanizes our differences, offering a counterbalance to the inhumanity often highlighted in

Western history. Through my photography, styling, and guidance, my contributions have been featured in some of the world's leading magazines, showing how creativity can deepen our connection to both home and one another.

The days following October 7th marked a turning point for me, a shift in how I understood the concept of home, both within ourselves and as a global collective. I know cameras and counterterrorism are worlds apart, but both demand a vision grounded in honesty, a willingness to see beyond oneself, and a commitment to fighting for truth through every possible angle and lens. Our legacy media has become a carrier of the mind virus—ignoring facts while siding with those who choose death over life.

From that day forward, the idea of home took on a deeper, more profound responsibility, one that has been woven into the pages that follow. It's why I traveled to a war-torn zone in order to make sense of the war at home.

WITNESS: ISRAEL, FEBRUARY 6TH, 2024

I was told not to be late, which felt like an impossible task in a country with no drip coffee. Or maybe that was just the spoiled American in me talking. I hurriedly finished putting on mascara and laced up my Converse, and headed downstairs to the King David Conference Room at the Dan Tel Aviv, determined to make it there early.

Surprisingly, I was the first to arrive.

My morning in Tel Aviv had started with crisp linens, the soft sound of the Mediterranean Sea, and a breakfast spread for a king. Despite the beauty, the air was thick with tension. Nerves were on edge. I took a bite of my breakfast, and could nearly taste the metallic aftertaste of hell—and I reminded myself why I was here.

This was the first of many trips to Israel as a selected delegate—an experience rooted in responsibility, not recognition. I was there to listen, to learn, and above all, to bear witness. In rooms filled with global leaders—many of whom choose to work quietly, without fanfare—I sat with the weight of stories that don't make headlines. The pursuit of peace in this region is both urgent and impossibly complex.

While Jews in Israel defend life on the ground and protect the state with their bodies and breath, we in the diaspora carry a different kind of responsibility. Speaking out comes with risk. It can feel heavy, even isolating. But it is not a burden—it is the bare minimum. And it pales in comparison to the real sacrifices being made by those on the front lines. This is the work. And it must be done with clarity, courage, and an unshakable commitment to truth. This is an inside view of what few see—but what the entire world needs to understand.

I dropped my bag onto a chair in the front row, because of course, I'm a nerd, a jet-lagged nerd, and scanned the room, my eyes darting around in desperate search for coffee. Thank goodness, a station was being set up in the back, its promise of caffeine a small mercy as I grappled with the eight-hour time difference, knowing it was midnight back home.

The space had that classic hotel conference room vibe: an abundance of neutral-toned carpet, the saltwater air carrying a faint humidity that battled an overworked AC, and a room versatile enough to host anywhere from forty to four hundred people, depending on the day's agenda. Just as I was about to make my move toward the coffee station, an olive-skinned man appeared to my right, startling me.

"Hi," he said, his voice soft but deliberate. It wasn't loud or commanding, yet it demanded my attention.

I was moved by the quiet intensity he carried. There was a depth in his eyes, framed by an unmistakable sadness, like someone bearing stories too heavy to share. It was hard to ignore, and for a moment, I questioned my decision to arrive so early.

He wore a shearling-collared jean jacket that reminded me of the one sitting in my closet back home. It was an unexpected detail, disarming in its ordinariness.

"Hi," I managed to reply, cursing the awkwardness creeping into my voice. He asked where I was from. His tone was casual, but I felt exposed, as if I might as well have been wearing a name tag reading "Hello, I'm American."

"And what do you do?" he continued.

"I'm a writer and photographer," I said, choosing my words carefully, trying to sound professional but not self-important.

His expression shifted, his sad eyes lighting up with interest. "What do you write about?"

"Creativity, mostly in the nonfiction space," I said, keeping my tone neutral, steering the focus away from myself.

A quiet smile touched his face. "I'm a writer too." His voice softened, carrying warmth that contrasted with the heaviness I'd seen earlier.

Curiosity piqued, I asked, "What do you write about?"

"Creativity in the military," he smiled.

It hit me then, that he wasn't just anyone. This was our speaker, the one scheduled to brief us today. The realization left me fumbling inwardly, though I tried to keep my composure.

I froze for a moment, nerves suddenly spiking. The coffee station in the back of the room, with its fresh brew and neatly stacked white cups, felt like a lifeline. With a polite smile, I excused myself, returning to my original objective: warm coffee, a steady presence, and an energetic start to the day.

As I filled my cup, I caught him smiling again out of the corner of my eye. More people had begun to fill the room, and the sadness I'd first noticed in his demeanor seemed to shift, replaced by something lighter, almost hopeful.

I took my seat in the front row, notebook in hand, ready to begin. This was the first of eight meetings that would leave a permanent mark on my mind and my heart.

When he approached the podium, it became clear he was more than a soldier. From a glance, he could have been mistaken for a father, a writer, or a CEO, roles that seemed to suit him as naturally as the uniform he still wears. But as he began to speak, those civilian titles receded, and the weight of his service emerged: this was a retired lieutenant colonel, still active in the reserves, embodying a responsibility that stretched beyond himself.

In Israel, not all heroes wear capes. Most wear the olive-green uniform of the Israel Defense Forces (IDF). Here, the extraordinary is woven into the fabric of daily life. Mandatory military service means that nearly every adult has, at some point, stood between the civilian world and an active war zone. Soldiers are sons and daughters, neighbors and classmates, artists, physicians, and engineers. They are ordinary people called to extraordinary roles, balancing the weight of national security with the pursuit of personal dreams.

He was no exception. His uniform was not just a symbol of service; it was a testament to the dualities the society holds, warriors or Lions of Judea, while at the same time existing as complex human beings doing the best they can. The paradox of a nation both vibrant and resilient, yet perpetually under siege.

As he spoke, it became clear that his service wasn't just about duty; it was about survival, the survival of his family, his neighbors, and his country. He represented a society where everyone, in their own way, becomes a hero. Some serve on the front lines, while others ensure that life continues in the face of uncertainty. His voice cut through the room, distinct and weary, carrying the weight of countless retellings. I wondered how many days, how many times, he had been asked to relive his service.

He told us stories of bravery, of defeat, of terror, of guilt from lives lost, unable to be saved. Stories of ambushes, where terrorists disguised in IDF uniforms unleashed chaos. And then, the story of October 7th, how he left his home, returning to his base to mobilize others and help repel the endless wave of terrorists who breached the border.

He looked like he hadn't slept in years, his face etched with exhaustion and resolve. Yet his words carried a powerful message, one that struck with unflinching clarity: objective evil exists. For those of us in the West, insulated by oceans and peace, his reminder was stark and sobering: if we don't wake up, the West is next.

What struck me most was his opening introduction into a conversation on "perspective," inviting those in the room to challenge their own.

His approach resonated with me on a professional level. His method of analyzing military strategy challenged every possible angle, considering the enemy's strengths and weaknesses while balancing the weight of lives at stake. It was a systematic approach rooted in discipline and clarity.

As I reflected on his words, I saw a parallel to my own craft. With the utmost respect, and without reducing the weight of centuries of military history and complex strategies of war, I've found that being a good photographer requires a similar mindset. To tell a story through the lens, you must challenge perspective, exhaust every angle, and remain relentless until the truth of the frame emerges.

Words from the morning followed me as I made my way throughout the day, eventually leading me into a small security screening room with very large video screens.

We traveled south to the city of Sderot, 800 meters from Gaza. Sderot is known as the bomb-shelter capital of the world, where innocent civilians and refugees in this city have fifteen seconds or less to seek shelter when the sirens sound.

Upon arrival, I was instructed to leave my phone in the car and refrain from geotagging my location for our collective safety. I was escorted into a worn building, a world dominated by machine guns, conference rooms, surveillance screens, cigarette butts, and a palpable tension in the air.

As I stepped into this environment, I became instinctively protective of the energy around me, bracing myself for what would unfold on the wall-to-wall screens. I centered myself in the space, grounding my presence to avoid detaching from my physical body, a trauma response or perhaps a coping mechanism (depending on the day) I had developed in childhood.

In doing so, I etched the scene into my memory: the white, scuffed walls, empty paper coffee cups stained with stress, worn floors that had seen countless feet, phones ringing endlessly, the harsh glare of fluorescent lights, and the small window behind me, its iron bars and opaque glass casting a dim, almost suffocating view.

But nothing could have prepared me for what I saw flickering across one of the forty video screens: the private replaying of raw footage of the war unfolding before us.

There are things you see in life that become part of your personality. This was one of those moments. As the video streams converged into one, amid the ringing of phones, I watched a small black car navigate its way across the top of the screen, surrounded by lush green trees and bathed in the warm golden glow of sunlight, anchored by a peaceful roundabout.

The images were from October 7th.

A family was in the black car, a mother, father, and their two young children. I could only imagine where they were going—perhaps dinner, home, or maybe even a playground.

Suddenly, the sirens blared, and the small black car stopped in the middle of the road.

The father reacted swiftly, jumped out of the car, clutching his four-year-old son tightly to his chest as he sprinted toward the nearest shelter.

The little boy's feet were swaying with each stride the father took to safety. In an instant, a speeding white truck appeared, circling the roundabout. There were men branded in green headbands hoisting guns in the air, filling the bed of the truck and hanging off the sides.

The looming threat of a bomb disappeared as these radicalized men roared past the black car, and sprayed the family with bullets.

Tears welled in my eyes, my shoulders tightened, and it was hard to breathe through the unfolding of this harrowing scene. I had no words for what my eyes saw, which echoed countless stories from the preceding months leading up to this afternoon.

The four-year-old boy made his way out from beneath the weight of his father's lifeless body and stood there, unsteady, on his two little feet. I drew a deep, shuddering breath.

His mother was dead in the car.

The terrorist ambush persisted throughout the city of Sderot on the 7th, where bullets were much heavier than bombs, and not even the friendly animal-shaped bomb shelters intentionally designed within playgrounds could save the innocent lives lost.

The sight of that child, thrust into a world without the comforting presence of his parents, remains etched in my mind, a poignant reminder of the unfathomable loss endured on that harrowing day. No matter how hard I try, I will never not think of him.

As I stepped out of the screening room and into the fresh air, a thick, heavy cloud of cigarette smoke hit me, from a group of female soldiers on break. Watching them, the weight of guilt settled over me, guilt for the privileges I've long taken for granted in the United States, the freedoms I've enjoyed without question, and the peace of mind I've known, untouched by the daily threats of terror they face. When I thanked them for their courage and service, their tired yet resilient smiles pierced through me, a stark reminder of the true meaning of privilege.

Privilege is safety.

In the afternoon, Mayor Alon Davidi briefed us on the realities of Sderot. His poignant definition of winning the war was to "see our children playing on playgrounds without fear," which highlights the essence of real privilege.

Davidi's unwavering dedication to rebuild the evacuated city of Sderot shed light on a truth that has long resonated with me, especially as I observe the discourse in the West. Here in the West, we find ourselves amid a propaganda war, and I stand on the digital front lines. The term "privilege" often feels like a grenade hurled into conversations from the "progressive woke" left. It's loaded with accusatory shrapnel, with "white" as the trigger of shame and "privilege" as the explosive core, unleashing a barrage of expletives meant to silence and divide.

It took these events in my life to wake up and gain the courage to push back on holding superficial differences like skin color over individual merit as a form of privilege or shame.

The color of my skin wouldn't have protected me from the acts on October 7th. My skin wasn't much of a shield from the global calls of jihad that have since followed.

My skin wouldn't have eased the fear of the communities who have been the targets of countless bomb threats and Molotov cocktails directed at our synagogues, temples, and schools in our American cities.

If my skin is supposed to equal protection and privilege, then why do over 91 percent of Jews feel unsafe, as reported by the American Jewish Committee (AJC)?

In 2025, the AJC's "State of Antisemitism in America" report found that one out of two Jewish Americans are changing their behavior to avoid antisemitism.[8] From removing Mezuzahs, Kippahs, and Magen David necklaces, to avoiding posting Jewish-related content online, or even changing their names on ridesharing apps like Uber and Lyft. These precautions may seem excessive, but they're understandable when you hear about incidents like Jews being abducted at New York airports simply for being Jews. I've personally experienced this rise in anti-Jewish sentiment directly, losing a major book deal after October 7th because my focus on social media switched from homes to Hamas.

The privilege pandemic presents several challenges here. First, it highlights a tendency toward simplistic thinking, providing a convenient excuse for those with agendas to dismiss historical context. There's a widespread desire to showcase one's morality without truly embodying its principles. This performative morality, often applied to strangers' privilege without sufficient understanding, not only exacerbates divisions in society, but also serves as a significant distraction from more pressing issues, such as wealth inequality.

Throughout history Jews have never been afforded the "privilege" of being perceived as white, not even once. The Jewish community is incredibly diverse, encompassing individuals of every hue, color, and creed known to humanity, while making up less than 1 percent of the global population.

Second, it conveniently overlooks personal history. And no, I'm not referring to the sins of your father, though, if I were, I'd likely be in hot water myself, considering mine is a certified degenerate.

Allow me to paint a picture of my family dynamic: picture my dad, a New York Jew, a gambler, perpetually in trouble with the IRS, who broke his first bookie at sixteen. He was an emotionally abusive alcoholic, and in one of his brighter moments decided to buy his girlfriend a flashy red Mustang he couldn't afford, all while possibly still being married to my mother.

When their relationship tanked, guess who ended up with the wheels, discovering a twenty-four-pack of Natural Light rolling around in the trunk? Yours truly, at the ripe age of seventeen, amid a ton of family drama and insecurities lurking in the back seat. Oh, and did I mention he turned their divorce into an eight-year soap opera, leaving us with more moves than *The Queen's Gambit* and enough financial uncertainty to make a Wall Street analyst sweat?

The point is this: I am not my father, thank goodness, and neither are you. You shouldn't have to carry the baggage of your forefathers while striving to be a thoughtful, courageous, and contributing human in this world. It's crucial to be mindful of where we come from, take stock of economic advantages, and try to create paths that contribute to our collective healing.

Real privilege, in this scenario, is emerging from an intact, healthy family home, with present parents making intentional choices and creating environments where children can thrive and grow up with meaning, values, and purpose. Real privilege in this scenario is having the safety to make choices for your future without being predicated or constrained by your past.

Third, despite my fair "privileged" skin, a result of centuries of persecution, pogroms, and exiles that forced my ancestors from the Middle East to Eastern Europe, our collective skin in the United States doesn't shield us from the war between two cultures we find ourselves entrenched in. Vegetius said it best: "If you want peace, prepare for war." This ideological conflict demands victory through deradicalization via education and reclaiming the center in our society.

EDUCATION THROUGH DERADICALIZATION

Less than two years and a few trips to Israel later, I'd step onto a stage to receive the Anti-Defamation League's Heroes Against Hate award.

David Schwimmer introduced me along with my friend and fellow honoree Adela Cojab Moadeb. Adela, an attorney who had recently returned from a conference in Berlin, spoke with me that evening about deradicalization and the power of reeducation.

"What was your biggest takeaway from the conference?" I asked her.

Her takeaway from Berlin struck me: before a society can begin to deradicalize, it must first accept defeat.

That's what happened in Germany after World War II. The country didn't just move on—it prepared for peace through education.[9] Their entire national consciousness was reshaped, ensuring that Nazism could never take root again.[10]

Now compare that to the Palestinian territories. No such reckoning has taken place. No acknowledgment of failure, no acceptance of defeat, no rejection of violent ideologies, no widespread effort to teach the next generation a different path.[11] Without that, the cycle continues.[12] We, as a global community, must take note of societies that refuse to accept defeat. Where Islamist ideologies not only persist, but actively counter the principles of safety, security, and prosperity for all.

Democracy is fragile. Nations that fail to pass down their core values risk watching them erode within a generation. When radicalization takes root and hostility festers, the only true antidote is a zero-tolerance policy with consequences and rigorous education. Without it, the cycle continues, deepening the divide.

A few months prior to the ADL event, I was in New York for UN Diplomacy Week, and had the opportunity to hear from Dr. Ali Rashid

Al Nuaimi, the chairman of the Defense, Interior, and Foreign Affairs Committee of the United Arab Emirates Federal National Council. Al Nuaimi was part of shepherding the 2020 Abraham accords, and he stressed the important role moral education would have in brokering real peace:

> The urgent need for a thorough reformation of religious education is underscored by global challenges brought on by violence and extremism committed in the name of religion. UAE responds to this problem by promoting a more contemporary interpretation of religious doctrines. The goal is to promote understanding and adapt religious education to modern contexts and not to change the fundamental principles of faith. Collaboration between experts from different fields ensures the creation of an inclusive and progressive religious education model that encourages dialogue, tolerance, and open mindedness. UAE's dedication to battling extremism and fostering a culture of peace and cooperation is demonstrated by this initiative.[13]

Education is crucial in determining a person's beliefs and attitudes. Reforming religious education is crucial to fostering tolerance, respect for diversity, and peaceful coexistence in the face of global challenges like terrorism and violent extremism.

Muslim communities must create their own interpretations of Islam that incorporate their cultural values in order to promote a sense of homeland pride while upholding religious principles. Societies can combat extremism and raise a generation that values moderation, conversation, and patriotism by implementing a contemporary approach to religious education.

As a bearer of complex identities, I know that neither my skin color nor any label assigned to me would protect me from the evils that too many in this country excuse or defend. Privilege is safety, the quiet luxury of never having to confront the depths of real danger in this world. But safety is not a right—it is a fragile construct, defended by those willing to name reality as it is, not as an ideology that distorts the truth. The world has seen what happens when evil is permitted to masquerade as righteousness, when terror rebrands itself as resistance, when victimhood is used to shield the guilty.

History does not bend toward justice on its own. It is bent by those with the courage to hold the line, to expose the lie, to demand truth. If our civilization is to stand, then those who seek to destroy it must be defeated. Not debated, not reasoned with, but disarmed, dismantled, and made to reckon with the weight of their own atrocities. And only then can we speak of reeducation, rebuild what was broken, and create lasting security and prosperity for all.

It's time to P.A.C.E. ourselves.

P.A.C.E.

A REFLECTIVE AND INTERACTIVE DISCUSSION GUIDE FOR BOOK CLUBS

Privilege Is Safety

Privilege isn't just wealth or comfort. It's security. It's waking up without fear. It's being able to walk outside, practice your faith, be unapologetically who you are, speak your truth—without threat. Not everyone has that privilege. And in the aftermath of October 7th, 2023, we're reminded just how fragile safety can be, and how quickly the world can turn a blind eye.

We're not just here to discuss—we're here to reflect, and to decide what responsibility we hold when safety becomes a privilege rather than a right. Try the prompts and exercises below with your book club or reading group—and allow space for both discomfort and discovery. Let this be more than a conversation; let it be a catalyst.

P PAUSE

Personal Reflection Exercise: Ask each member of your group to close their eyes and sit with the following prompts. Take five minutes and share with the group:

- What did safety mean to you growing up?
- When have you taken your own peace and security for granted?
- When have you felt fear—for yourself, your family, your community?
- What does it feel like to sit in the discomfort of seeing others' safety stolen?
- Write down a moment when you realized safety isn't guaranteed for everyone. How did it shift your perspective?

A ANALYZE

Group Discussion: Who Shapes Privilege Narratives?

Peggy McIntosh's 1988 essay, "White Privilege: Unpacking the Invisible Knapsack," identified unearned advantages tied to race. However, her framework has been critiqued for confusing class privilege with race privilege, often blurring the lines between economic status and racial identity.

In the current climate, the privilege narrative has shifted from a tool for self-awareness to one that silences dissenting voices. The same institutions that define privilege—media, academia, cultural influencers—often shape whose suffering is seen and whose is erased. This is especially true when it comes to Jewish experiences, where issues of safety and historical trauma are ignored.

Discussion Questions

- How has the term "privilege" evolved in your lifetime?
- Who benefits when privilege discourse silences certain voices, especially Jewish voices?
- When the media frames acts of terrorism as "resistance," what's at stake for truth?
- How do you personally assess the sources you trust and whose voices you believe?

C CONTEMPLATE

Group Reflection: The Cost of Truth-Telling

The images and stories from the October 7th Hamas attacks were meant to paralyze the Jewish people—to instill fear, grief, and silence. But what if refusing silence is the ultimate act of resistance?

Safety is a privilege. What does it mean to bear witness in a world that rewards terror with sympathy? What does it cost to stand up for truth—and are we willing to pay it?

Discussion Questions

- What does it mean to you to "bear witness"—in your family, in your community, or online?
- Have you ever hesitated to speak up because of fear, of backlash, loss, alienation?
- Where do you personally draw the line between safety and courage?
- What price are you willing to pay for truth—and what price feels too high?

E ENGAGE

Let's each commit to one action—large or small—to elevate truth, challenge sanitization, and stand for those whose safety has been stripped.

Group Brainstorming Ideas

- Share firsthand testimonies from October 7th survivors.
- Write letters to media outlets demanding accurate coverage.
- Support journalists and historians preserving objective truths.
- Attend rallies, vigils, or educational events focused on Jewish safety.
- Engage with foreign policy: educate yourself on the global fight against Islamic jihad and its implications on Western security.

Recommended Resources

- The Foundation for Defense of Democracies, FDD.org[14]
- Douglas Murray's book *The War on the West*[15]
- Ayaan Hirsi Ali's book *Heretic: Why Islam Needs a Reformation Now*[16]

CHAPTER 2

SITTING SHIVA FOR DEI, BUH-BYE

I kept inching my chair over, bit by bit, and pretended I wasn't the one speaking today. Public speaking used to terrify me, and I still feel the remnants of those nerves. I'd go into full Old School blackout mode, Will Ferrell–style, every time I hit the stage.

I've grown more and more comfortable with speaking by focusing on the message, not myself—it's about channeling something bigger than my fear. Still, on this particular day, my energy was running on empty, and the thought of being "on" felt heavier than usual.

Behind me, women stood pressed against the walls, and the shuffling of their body language made it visibly obvious there weren't enough seats. My mind raced through potential solutions: I could stand and channel my inner TED Talk energy, though the cozy setting begged for something less formal. I could offer my seat, scout for a stool, or maybe just give in to gravity and dissolve into the Oushak rug, which looked far more inviting than it had any right to be.

The setting was a private living room in the South. Afternoon light streamed through tall windows, casting a soft, golden glow that could make even the late Diane Keaton jealous. Around me, women leaned forward in their seats, perched on couches and ottomans, eager to discuss the state of the world, and so we did.

I'd traveled in from Nashville the day before to speak at a fundraiser. Instead of heading home first thing in the morning, I'd been easily persuaded to stay for a smaller, more intimate gathering, exactly the kind I love and thrive in. The faces were new, but the questions were old, ones I'd been fielding for more than a year: "What can we do about the media?" "How do we combat misinformation?" "How can we actually make a difference?" "What were your takeaways from Israel?"

And then, just as I was settling into the comforting rhythm of predictability, a voice sliced through the polite, circular chatter like a needle scratching a record.

A woman sat in a cozy upholstered chair, relaxed and reclined, radiating a calm confidence that commanded attention. With a measured, steady tone, she raised her hand and locked eyes with me.

I smiled and nodded, inviting her to speak.

"You don't look Jewish," she began, her tone light but deliberate, "so I'm sure you assimilate well with your blonde hair and blue eyes. I'm curious, what opportunities has your privilege afforded you?"

I looked at her, gauging the room's temperature. The silence was thick, my adrenaline inviting me to lean into the truth, my truth.

"You know," I began, my voice steady but thoughtful, "if we're going to talk about privilege, let's start with safety, real safety. Because I didn't have it growing up. My parents went through an eight-year divorce that made *The War of the Roses* look like a lighthearted rom-com. I witnessed my father drinking heavily, popping pills, gambling, raging against walls, banisters, and brawling in bars. We moved homes constantly. There was financial instability, I witnessed physical violence, and pure chaos."

I paused, letting the weight of those words settle.

I could hear my heart beating, and I could feel the women's thoughts scanning me, searching for cracks despite how put together I looked. This was a room apologizing for its success—but I refused. I don't apologize for resilience. When things break, I don't just piece them back together; I make them stronger. I will not submit to the oppression Olympics. That's not a podium I want to stand on, nor will I accept. Because I don't play by those rules. I never have. I build. I rise. And I do it on my own terms.

"You asked what opportunities I've had because of privilege," I answered. "No, I am going to tell you about the opportunities lost—ones I paid my dues for, built a business around, worked hard for, became a leader in, earned, and naturally deserved. From TV projects I was passed over because networks were filling BIPOC quotas—only purchasing Black and brown leads—to the moment in 2022 that broke my spirit."

I looked out at the crowd and told the following story.

In 2022, I was set to have the front cover feature of the most coveted design magazine, and in my opinion the gold standard in architecture and design. Here's what that meant to me: it was the culmination of decades of work, tens of thousands of hours spent serving my clients, editing, endless miles traveling and honing my craft to become one of the best in the country. Double-digit online features in Condé Nast publications, but never in print, the outlet that was the gold standard for my niche. The home in question? A beautiful space I styled with my designer client for a country music star whose brand is this ethereal country-meets-cosmic-cowgirl vibe, with a doobie and a dose of Dolly.

I shared the gallery of photos with her team , and they loved them. Not long after I developed the pitch, I found out that my gallery—exactly as I had shot it—had been approved by the editor-in-chief for print. The Cosmic Cowgirl's home would be the May 2022 front cover. This was a milestone I had worked so hard for, and I was beyond grateful—not just for myself, but for my client, too.

But then, at the last moment, the songbird's team apparently pulled me from the feature. They didn't even tell me; I was ghosted.

Then I saw it.

I still get sick to my stomach thinking about this.

I was in the car, scrolling through Instagram in a parking lot, when I stopped cold—what the hell? The designer was posting behind-the-scenes shots of the space, and it looked like a reshoot was happening. Same flowers, same props, same staging with a few trivial alterations. Once a project is accepted by an outlet, this kind of thing is discouraged and unnecessary—one, because we already did the work and two, we don't want to spoil the surprise for readers.

As I kept scrolling, the unease grew. The frames, the styling, the setup—it was all too familiar for comfort. But I wasn't the one behind the lens.

I emailed. I texted. Silence.

Weeks later, I finally got the designer on the phone. She was vague, dodging my questions, but the truth was clear: despite my gallery being approved and accepted, the house was being photographed again. And I had been cut out.

WHY?!

I wrote the team:

> I only assume the decision to go with another photographer wasn't based on talent, so being excluded from the reshoot is both personally and professionally devastating. Moreover, as the owner of the original gallery, the risk of copyright infringement is high once the publication has approved it, and the decision to use another photographer creates two competing galleries in the marketplace.

When the magazine itself arrived in my mailbox, I felt sick. I couldn't even bring myself to look at it.

I want to make this abundantly clear: the editorial team had my photos in hand for weeks before making the decision to fly in a photographer—into my own backyard, to the home just minutes from where I lived—to reshoot the project. And based on the striking similarities of her images, I can only assume the photographer had full access to my work. The front cover confirmed it. The framing, the composition—the entire gallery—were uncomfortably similar to my shots, with only a floral here or a step stool there added. My work had been used as a template, but my name was nowhere to be found.

The country star had just been featured on the cover of *TIME* for her work toward a more "equal" world. They chose a Black photographer from the Bronx, who typically doesn't work in interiors, but is focused on Black and brown communities. She had recently photographed Supreme Court Justice Ketanji Brown Jackson.

I couldn't comprehend them stepping on the neck of someone who comes from one of the most historically persecuted groups to amplify someone who doesn't even work in my niche. However, this was the charade they were selling, and I wasn't wrong.

The decision about the work was about optics. My gallery was used as a template. My frames, my vision—reflected through another lens.

And just like that, I wasn't even part of the conversation. I was exiled. The feature debuted in the summer, and there was my frame, now with someone else's name. The photographer never promoted the feature on her social media. I couldn't help but wonder if it was because the country star was too porcelain, or if, perhaps, it simply didn't mean much to the photographer or her demographic.

After I shared this story, I allowed the weight of the words to sink into the room, glancing around to meet their eyes before continuing.

This lost feature wasn't just about my white skin. It was about the message it sends when a box gets checked purely for appearances—and how that sidelines the quality of the work itself. Did the photographer know? Judging by the similarities, I'd have to assume so. The conversation with my copyright attorney was summed up with an analogy: it's like a music producer finishing an album, only to have someone else put their name on it. I didn't pursue legal action, not because it wasn't in my purview, but because it was David going up against Goliath. Regardless, checking boxes often matters more than being hired for talent—because nothing says "progress" like turning artists into demographic racial data points.

DEI claims to champion equity and inclusion. But when skin color becomes the ticket and talent is left backstage, that's not justice. That's just performance. All shimmer, no soul. They called it progress, but it felt more like betrayal—wrapped in pastel rhinestones and set to a Golden Hour soundtrack. A prettier picture, sure. Just not an honest one.

I paused, taking a breath before continuing with more conviction.

"The truth is," I said to the room, "DEI isn't fostering inclusion; it's creating new divisions. It's asking us to see each other not for who we are or what we've built, but for what box we check. And in doing so, it's teaching us to withhold compassion, understanding, and connection from one another; it teaches us to step on the neck of another. That's not equality. That's just a different form of exclusion."

I scanned the room and softened further.

"What I want to offer here isn't anger, it's a challenge. We need to move beyond this. Beyond the binary of oppressed and oppressor. Beyond labels and hierarchies. We need to return to what Dr. King taught us: to judge one another by the content of our character. Not as an afterthought, but as the guiding principle for how we live, lead, and connect."[17]

I concluded: "That's how we dismantle this ideology, not with bitterness, but with profound clarity and conviction. By showing what's possible when we meet one another with integrity. That's the only way forward. And it's worth fighting for."

I looked at the women's faces after I told my story and could sense their openness. They were receptive. There was no hostility.

I left the event feeling grateful for an opportunity to be a resource for women who are asking hard questions.

(Oh and by the way, the cosmic cowgirl wasn't thrilled with DEI when Beyoncé took home the Grammy for Best Country Album of the Year. How do I know? Her sour reaction went viral. Google it.)

THE BROKEN PROMISE OF DEI

Growing up in Oklahoma and spending much of my adult life in the South, I've witnessed both the progress made and the lingering tension around racial and cultural differences. These issues were not confined to a history book. These experiences have impacted my career and fueled my commitment to helping rebuild a collective center.

Yet in the very industries where my photos and words have found their home—media, editorial, wellness, and design—the stark contradictions have become impossible to ignore. These spaces, which proudly champion tolerance and inclusion, often suppress diversity of thought, reducing inclusion to a rigid, righteous binary and judging individuals solely based on immutable characteristics. This approach is not just flawed; it is a betrayal of the very principles DEI claims to champion.

A few things happened when my first book, *The New Southern Style*, was published in September 2020.

First, I accidentally created the design industry's first inclusive coffee-table book, written and photographed through the lens of a deeply Jewish principle: our social responsibility to one another. I wanted every little girl to be able to see herself in its pages—to know she could be the architect of her own life. That life pivots yield growth. That creativity connects us to community. That belonging can be built.

Second, I was silenced by legacy media because of my immutable characteristics. Too white. Too blonde. Too much of a Jew.

Third, I was called "racist" and "white" far more times than I could have imagined. Often by people influenced by arguments of antiracist evangelists such as Ibram X. Kendi's (born Ibram Henry Rogers) in *How to Be an Antiracist*; Robin DiAngelo's concepts from *White Fragility*; Layla F. Saad's principles of *Become an Antiracist Changemaker*; and Rachel Cargle's coaching from her formerly titled book *I Don't Want Your Love and Light*.

It was also during this time that I witnessed our shared human morality being outsourced and enforced through three simple letters: D.E.I.

My work was anchored in principles tied to my Judaism, particularly the concept of tikkun olam, or repairing the world. It was rooted in something universal that exists within all of us: our light, our creativity, and the transformative power of building bridges side by side through innovation, education, and a vision for a better future.

I've seen how good intentions tied to rigid narrative turn people into stereotypes, suppress diverse ideas, and create division instead of unity.

Beyond wanting every little girl to see herself in the pages of my first book, I wanted to inspire the dreamers, especially those who came from less-than-ideal circumstances, or who faced life pivots, to take a chance on their lives. I wanted them to wake up and realize that they hold the power to become the architects of their own stories, to step into their courage and co-create with hope, rather than being swept away by the tides of circumstance. My goal was for the book to ignite bravery and creativity, to remind everyone that no matter where we start, we have the ability to shape our own paths. That vision became my North Star, and still is a deeply held desire to create something authentic and meaningful, not performative or calculated.

I didn't write and photograph *The New Southern Style* to gain approval or access to certain progressive circles. I penned the book long before the George Floyd riots of 2020 and the societal upheaval that followed his death, but by the time it was released, American cities were burning, and divisions were deepening.

Friends of mine, who simply wanted to protect their small female-owned businesses from senseless destruction, were unfairly branded as racists.

One friend in particular, who owns a store in a shopping center, was targeted. Rumors of Antifa targeting local small businesses and plans to burn buildings, similar to those seen in other cities, led to the entire shopping center being boarded up.

The timing couldn't have been worse. It was barely weeks after businesses reopened following pandemic lockdowns that devastated so many small businesses. The shop was empty, and my friend, returning from her grandfather's funeral, had one of her employees put up a sign reading: 24-Hour Audio and Video Surveillance. All Valuable Items Removed From the Premises.

My friend owned a jewelry store filled with delicate everyday pieces, but the atmosphere was anything but delicate. Among the social media messages urging her to "stay safe," there was also a flood of criticism. Accusations of failing to post a sign "to support change and amplify Black voices," and even claims that "looting isn't reckless or unwarranted."

The hypocrisy was glaring: instead of rallying around vulnerable, small, female-owned businesses, the focus shifted to justifying destruction with performative demands, offering no solutions and causing further harm. Meanwhile, those loudly advocating for dismantling systems of oppression often reaped the rewards while the communities they claimed to serve were left behind.

This climate, where race hustling overshadowed merit and critical thinking, stood in direct contrast to everything my book represented. *The New Southern Style* was built on a foundation of community, creativity, and connection. It was a celebration of resilience and humanity, not a performative statement catering to the chaos of the moment.

The book sought to bridge divides, not exploit them, and to inspire meaningful change rooted in empathy and shared understanding, not hollow virtue signaling or the frenzy that left so many real needs unmet.

The veil has been lifted, revealing a troubling reality: what once symbolized fairness and inclusion has devolved into a system that fosters inequity, where "DEI" might as well stand for "Didn't Earn It." This shift undermines the core values of merit, individual dignity, and critical thought, replacing them with hollow tokenism and performative virtue. Such erosion strikes at the heart of what makes the United States a beacon of opportunity, innovation, and freedom.

THE EVOLUTION OF DEI: FROM FAIRNESS TO FRACTURE

Where the Biden-Harris administration enabled this chaos, the Trump administration is taking decisive action to dismantle this ideology and restore a system built on merit—one where we are judged by our work, not by identity politics. However, much like most conspiracy theories, DEI is a shape-shifting agenda, constantly rebranding itself into whatever acronym fits the narrative of the moment. Be wary of all CRTs, BLMs, DEIs, and BDSs, because not only are they BS, but they are contemporary Marxism in disguise.

DEI programs are the Fyre Festival of inclusion: they sold a glamorous vision of equity and progress but delivered exclusion, hostility, authoritarian behavior, and an $8 billion industry of unmet promises. Beneath the hype lies a reality that fails to deliver on its lofty ideals.

At its core, DEI began with noble intentions to create a more just society. The Civil Rights Movement, the passage of the Civil Rights Act in 1964, and the push for affirmative action in the 1970s were all about breaking down barriers and ensuring that people of color had access to the same opportunities as their white counterparts.[18] That was the promise: a vision of a world where no one would be held back because of the color of their skin, their gender, or their background.[19]

For a while, DEI focused on just that: equal access, representation, and the dismantling of barriers.[20] We saw more women in leadership roles. We saw greater diversity in the workforce and academia.[21] We saw changes in laws and policies that gave previously marginalized groups more of a voice and a place at the table. While these strides were significant, something shifted over time. Instead of focusing on equal access for all, DEI prioritized identity politics and lazy binaries, while excluding Jews.

THE PROBLEM WITH IDENTITY POLITICS

As DEI evolved, its focus shifted from opportunity to identity. In many ways this was a response to the complexity of human experience; it recognized that the intersection of race, gender, and class could create unique challenges.[22] But it also gave rise to new problems. Rather than embracing the richness of individual identities, DEI programs started compartmentalizing people into two groups: oppressed versus oppressor, powerless versus powerful, colonized versus colonizer, Black versus white. Resources and attention were increasingly allocated based on one's "perceived" level of oppression.[23]

The issue? This binary framework of oppressors and oppressed doesn't tell the full story. It oversimplifies the complexities of identity and, in many cases, undermines the real struggles faced by communities in need. For example, within this framework, Jews are often dismissed because they don't fit neatly into the narrative of "oppressed" groups.

Despite being one of the smallest populations, with only 16 million Jews worldwide, and one of the most persecuted groups in history, Jews face real challenges. In 2024, the FBI reported that anti-Jewish hate crimes reached the highest number ever recorded, rising 5.8 percent from 2023.[24] This continued a dramatic upward trend: in 2023, anti-Jewish hate crimes had risen 63 percent from 2022. In the United States, Jews make up roughly 2 percent of the population, yet account for nearly 70 percent of religion-based hate crimes, according to the FBI.[25]

Additionally, according to the DEI binary, the Jewish community is deemed to be "white," even though Jews have historically never been categorized as such and have been persecuted for not being part of the "white" race; hello, Hitler.[26]

And if you think I am sounding the alarm bells too early: a study put out in November 2024 by Network Contagion Research Institute and Rutgers University suggested that DEI pedagogy can actually have unintentional negative consequences that create hostility and support for extreme views of race.[27]

The West needs to be ending extremism, not fueling it.

During one experiment, researchers presented participants with quotes from Adolf Hitler, but swapped the word "Jew" for "Brahmin," which is the highest class in India's caste system. Horrifyingly, the case study found an increase in agreement with Adolf Hitler's statements:

> Participants exposed to DEI content were markedly more likely to endorse Hitler's demonization statements, agreeing that

> Brahmins are "parasites" (+35.4%), "viruses" (+33.8%), and "the devil personified" (+27.1%) (see supplement for exact quotes). These findings suggest that exposure to anti-oppressive narratives can increase the endorsement of the type of demonization and scapegoating characteristic of authoritarianism.

This oversimplification harms everyone. It erases the lived experiences of Jews and other marginalized communities, reducing them to mere statistics rather than recognizing the full depth of their identities. And, as we see more and more, this binary logic breeds division instead of unity. Rather than fostering understanding, it pits people against each other in a battle for the title of "most oppressed" or "us versus them."

THE EXCLUSION OF JEWS IN DEI: WHY IT MATTERS AND WHY EVERYONE SHOULD CARE

As a Jewish woman, I find the exclusion of Jews from DEI conversations has become impossible to ignore. Once you recognize it, the "inclusion delusion" inherent in DEI frameworks becomes glaringly clear. Over the years, I've witnessed Jewish communities being sidelined—especially in workplaces, social settings, and educational institutions. Despite the alarming rise in antisemitism both in the United States and globally, DEI initiatives fail to address the unique challenges Jews face.[28]

THE PROBLEM OF ANTISEMITISM IN ACADEMIA

Take the growing problem of antisemitism on college campuses, for example. In a 2023 survey, the American Jewish Committee reported that one in four Jewish college students feared for their physical safety before attending campus amid rising tensions and violence. By 2024, that figure skyrocketed to three in four Jewish students fearing for their safety.[29] While Jewish students face increasing harassment and threats, DEI programs and university consultants are often silent, failing to respond with the urgency these issues demand.

A 2021 Heritage Foundation study examining the Twitter feeds of 741 DEI personnel at 65 universities found that the vast majority of their tweets about Israel were not only critical but veered into outright antisemitism.[30] The binary framework on which DEI operates does more than misalign with Western values; it inadvertently reinforces harmful anti-Jewish and anti-Israel narratives. DEI fails to recognize the specific forms of hatred directed at Jews, treating them as an afterthought, if at all.

Exclusion in the Workplace

But the exclusion of Jews goes beyond academia. In the workplace, 52 percent of Jewish employees report encountering antisemitism, with many feeling ignored by DEI initiatives. A 2023 survey by Resume Builder found that one in four hiring managers were unwilling to advance Jewish applicants, further marginalizing them in professional settings.[31]

In 2024, a study conducted by the ADL found that Jewish Americans need to submit 24 percent more job applications than their peers with Western European backgrounds for the same roles, while Israeli-Americans must submit 39 percent more.[32]

Cultural Exclusion and the Broader Impact

The problem extends into cultural spaces too, as seen with the global Jewish book ban of 2023, which targeted Israeli publishers and Jewish authors. I personally experienced this when I lost a major book deal as a result of this exclusionary trend. The publishing industry, driven by DEI frameworks, failed to acknowledge how these initiatives contributed to the marginalization of Jewish voices, often equating support for Israel with bigotry.

By the end of 2024, the numbers were undeniable: 46 percent of the global population harbored antisemitic beliefs, according to the ADL. With the world's population at 8.2 billion, this staggering figure translates to 3.73 billion people harboring hatred against Jews, a chilling reminder of how silence allows hate to take root and spread across the world.

The Dangerous Erasure of Jewish Identity

The exclusion of Jews from DEI frameworks isn't just a minor oversight, it's a deliberate erasure of Jewish identity, history, and contributions. This exclusion is being exploited by BDS (Boycott, Divestment, and Sanctions, a movement we'll discuss in detail later in this book) and allows antisemitism to thrive in spaces that claim to be inclusive, while failing to protect the communities most in need of support.

Throughout history, Jews have been racialized and targeted. During WWII, Jews were deemed an inferior race, resulting in genocide. Today, DEI frameworks perpetuate a disturbing mutation of this antisemitism by positioning Jews as a "white" and "privileged" group, erasing the historical and contemporary realities of Jewish history.

The very framework of DEI reinforces the same harmful ideologies that antisemitism thrives on: stereotyping, scapegoating, and exclusion. It silences Jewish voices, whitewashes our history, and perpetuates dangerous myths of superiority. This is not inclusion; it's betrayal.

Jews have faced centuries of intentional discrimination, from pogroms to the Holocaust and now a global resurgence of antisemitism. Yet DEI initiatives ignore this reality, which is not just an oversight; it's a framework that harms the very people it claims to protect.

Why Everyone Needs to Care

The Jewish community serves as a warning sign for society. We are the yellow light before it turns red. When antisemitism is low, it signals tolerance, a healthy democracy, and human decency.

It is the Jewish responsibility to serve as the barometer of a society's conscience. When our alarm bells go from yellow to red, people need to sit down and listen. History shows that intolerance often begins with the

Jews—but it rarely ends there. Ignoring the warning signs is a concern for us all.

The exclusion of Jews from DEI programs isn't just a Jewish issue. It's a human issue. A system that fails to protect one group from discrimination cannot be trusted to protect anyone. Silencing Jewish voices and experiences sets a dangerous precedent, eroding the very principles DEI claims to uphold.

To build a truly inclusive society, we must move beyond outdated frameworks. Real diversity and equality are achieved through education, freedom of speech, constructive disagreement, diversity of thought, active listening, skill-building, and merit—principles that foster unity instead of division. All groups, including Jews, must be recognized as equal participants in shaping a healthier, more just future.

P.A.C.E.

A REFLECTIVE + INTERACTIVE DISCUSSION GUIDE FOR BOOK CLUBS

Sitting Shiva for DEI, Buh-Bye

P PAUSE

Take a moment to reflect on the rise—and the unraveling—of Diversity, Equity, and Inclusion (DEI). In 2020, DEI was celebrated as the cornerstone of progress. Today, we're beginning to see the cracks: its limitations, contradictions, and the growing question of whether it truly serves the communities it claims to uplift. Within your book club or reading circle, sit with the following questions. Reflect honestly, even if it's uncomfortable:

- How has DEI shaped cultural, academic, and professional life over the past few years? Who benefited, and who has been left behind?
- Why is DEI dissolving, and what does this unraveling reveal about its foundational flaws or limitations?
- DEI, Critical Race Theory (CRT), and Cultural Marxism share similar ideological roots. As DEI fades from the mainstream, how might these frameworks adapt or evolve under different names or institutional banners?
- What do we stand to gain—intellectually, ethically, and communally—when we move beyond performative equity models? What might a more truthful and unifying alternative look like?

A ANALYZE

Group Discussion and Resources:

Will the focus on group identity continue to drive wedges between us, or could moving toward a colorblind society promote greater unity? It's crucial to evaluate whether DEI truly promotes equality or inadvertently deepens divisions.

To expand your understanding, explore the following resources:

- *The End of Race Politics: Arguments for a Colorblind Society* by Coleman Hughes.[33] Hughes makes a compelling case for prioritizing individual identity over group categories, offering a critique of race-based identity politics. You may also want to dive into his powerful TED Talk to hear how his arguments can contribute to a more unified society.
- "America Works, DEI Doesn't" (*Tablet* magazine, January 2024),[34] as a powerful critique of DEI programs, emphasizing how they may inadvertently divide people and undermine merit.
- "How DEI Is Supplanting Truth as the Mission of American Universities," (*The Free Press*, January 9, 2023)[35] explores how DEI's prioritization of ideological conformity over truth is damaging to academic freedom and intellectual diversity.
- *Woke Antisemitism* by David Bernstein[36] explores how woke ideologies, including DEI, can fuel antisemitism perpetuating anti-Jewish and anti-Israel narratives. Additionally, Bernstein is the founder of the North American Values Institute and is a tremendous resource to further support your curiosity.
- *Social Justice Fallacies* by Thomas Sowell[37] is a critical look at social justice ideologies, including their oversimplification of complex issues.

C CONTEMPLATE

As DEI crumbles under the weight of its own contradictions, we have an opportunity to build something better—a society in which people are seen as whole individuals, defined by their merit, values, and contributions, not by immutable traits.

Discussion Prompts:

- What if true equality meant honoring the complexity of each person, rather than reducing them to a box to check?
- Could we finally move beyond performative inclusivity to build a society rooted in fairness, intellectual freedom, and mutual respect?
- The fall of DEI isn't the end—it's a chance to create something far more authentic and just.

E ENGAGE

Engagement is not about passively accepting the current state—it's about questioning, pushing back, and actively pursuing change. Here's how to engage:

- **Challenge DEI Where You Are.** Don't just accept DEI programs. If you're involved in local government, school districts, or corporations, ask the hard questions. Is this really uniting us? Or is it dividing us further by forcing people into categories they didn't choose? Speak up and ask if these programs are more about virtue signaling than building genuine connections.
- **Make Room for Jewish Voices.** I don't believe in inclusion for the sake of optics. This isn't about checking boxes or performative equity. But during war, and in the most sensitive chapters of history, Jewish voices have not just been excluded—they've been erased. Too often, Jews are sidelined, blamed, or dismissed—*even as they're being targeted*. In moments of global reckoning, the Jewish perspective is missing from the town square and the proverbial table. That silence isn't just an oversight—it's a pattern. And it needs to end. Jewish voices are not an accessory to diversity; they are a vital part of the historical, ethical, and human landscape. Listen to them as you would any other source of wisdom,

context, and lived experience—especially when discussing justice, genocide, war, resilience, and what it means to survive.

- **Create Spaces for Real Dialogue.** Seek out and nurture spaces where tough, honest, and raw conversations can happen—without fear of societal or professional consequences. Whether it's a community gathering, a work meeting, or even a social media space, create environments where free speech and merit are protected and allowed to thrive.
- **Call Out Tokenism.** If you see diversity being used as a checkbox rather than a genuine effort to include, call it out. Tokenism doesn't help anyone—it's a shallow fix that prevents real change. Push for a world where people are valued for their character, values, and unique talents, not just for the category they belong to. Ask yourself: Are we truly valuing this person for their unique perspective or talent, or just using them to satisfy a societal narrative?
- **Educate, Share, and Challenge.** Don't sit on the sidelines. Equip yourself with knowledge and challenge the mainstream narrative. Start conversations that question the surface-level talking points. Encourage those around you to think critically and challenge the status quo, especially when it comes to group-based identity politics. The best place to start is with a question: What do you mean by this? Tell me more about that? Where did you get that information? How do you know that?
- **Create a Personal Commitment Card** (each group member writes and keeps one). I commit to: [name one or more specific actions from the above list, or brainstorm your own].
  - Example: "I will read *The End of Race Politics* by Coleman Hughes and share these resources with others to foster more thoughtful discussions about DEI and its impact."

    Carry your card with you as a reminder until you complete the task. Then write a new card!

CHAPTER 3

OBSESSION WITH OPPRESSION

> @InsertInstagramFollower: Happy Birthday! I love how you are always about building women up! Thank you for sharing! Hope 2020 is wonderful to you

It wasn't. It was a total shit show.

On December 31st, I planned to celebrate the remaining hours of 2019 with a birthday dinner party at my home.

That morning, I woke up with a rare and satisfying sense of completion—something I almost never experience on New Year's Eve.

My first manuscript was complete, my client work tidied up, and by evening, my house would come alive with laughter and the energy of thirteen of my closest girlfriends. I envisioned a night of meaningful conversations, thoughtful silences as we savored each bite, and the kind of warmth that lingers long after the last guest has left.

Before the world cracked open and chaos spilled out, creating and capturing beautiful spaces was what I did best. I called it "practical fantasy" when I was on set styling a house and photographing it for a client. Depending on the day, this work could feel like an antidote to the mounting anxiety of modern life . . . or like fuel for the neurotic perfectionism raging on Pinterest. That morning, I chose the antidote.

I sprang out of bed, poured myself a cup of coffee, and greeted the rental company at the door. Together, we carried in the long, matte-white tables, candles, glassware, and chairs. The tables fit the space between my kitchen and living room like they were designed just for this moment.

I began styling the tablescape, letting the process anchor me in the present. Down the center of the table, I placed candles of varying heights, creating a flickering glow that would later become the evening's quiet star.

Vibrant pink peonies wove through the candles like a conversation of their own, their petals soft and saturated. I set light-gray ceramic plates in front of each chair, perfectly aligned and paired with matching flatware. Linen napkins were tied into casual knots, striking that perfect balance between effortless and intentional.

At my parties, I always make sure every guest is greeted with a gift. Not just an object, but a gesture of connection.

That evening, the gift was twofold: a card featuring a conversation quote to spark depth and vulnerability, and a book, *Vibrate Higher Daily*, from a soon-to-be close friend, Lalah Delia. A small offering of inspiration to carry home with them.

As I stood back to take in the scene, I felt a wave of gratitude. Everything was exactly as I'd envisioned: seamless, warm, and brimming with promise before my guests arrived.

I began the playlist, Etta James singing softly in the background, just as I opened the door to my friend Ryan, who is a brilliant chef. Aromas began to fill the air as he worked, soon mingling with bursts of laughter and snippets of conversation as the first few friends arrived. The glow of candlelight set the tone, carrying the celebration of connection, creativity, and care late into the night as we seamlessly closed out 2019.

Life, however, has an interesting sense of irony, doesn't it?

Ten days later this "seamless" picture was a distant memory. The year 2020 unraveled into a barrage of catastrophes that shattered any sense of sanity.

It began with the Australian bushfires, an inferno so massive it turned skies blood orange, and made most apocalyptic movies look tame. In late January, Kobe Bryant, a global icon, a legend, was lost too soon, along with his daughter and seven others in a helicopter crash that stopped time for a moment.

Then came the COVID-19 pandemic, which swept across the globe like a vengeful storm, transforming hand sanitizer into currency and sweatpants into acceptable work attire.

Then, as we were adjusting to a world of face masks and Zoom calls, there were the murder hornets. Yes, *murder hornets*, because apparently 2020 needed to be extra dramatic. (Whatever happened to those, by the way?)

Meanwhile, wildfires ripped ferociously through the West Coast—like something out of a Biblical plague.

As if natural disasters weren't enough, the country erupted in Black Lives Matter protests—a nationwide reckoning over race and alleged police brutality that swept through our cities, institutions, and collective consciousness. Calls to defund the police ignited fierce debate, crime rates surged, and the ideological divide widened into a chasm that felt impossible to bridge.

While Black Americans make up roughly 14 percent of the US population, they are involved in a disproportionately higher percentage of violent crime arrests and police interactions.[38]

When adjusting for these factors, multiple peer-reviewed studies—including research from Harvard economist Roland Fryer—have found no racial bias in police use of lethal force. In short, the data shows that police do not disproportionately shoot Black Americans once context is accounted for.[39] These findings contradict the dominant cultural narrative in 2020 that Black Americans are disproportionately and systematically hunted by police. Yes, racial disparities exist in America—and should be addressed with care and seriousness. But when emotion overrides facts, the result is not justice. It's distortion and it is damaging for others.

My book was released into a turbulent world, just weeks after George Floyd's death—a moment that cast a long shadow over everything. What should have been a celebratory achievement felt surreal instead. A carefully planned eleven-city book tour dissolved into a haze of shelter-in-place orders, virtual events, and a silence cast so heavily over those who looked like me that it made me question everything, even the value of my own efforts. At the time, I wondered if common sense had taken a long, indefinite vacation.

The year everything changed marked the dawn of a cultural shift that singled out white women for collective shame and silencing. For Jews, who have historically been excluded from the category of "white," this added yet another layer of erasure.

But that nuance didn't matter to figures like Rachel Cargle and Austin Channing Brown, whose business model thrived on public shaming and naming and turning legitimate questions into spectacles of humiliation. Their assertions weren't conversations; they were orchestrated takedowns that cultivated fear and silence, creating an environment where even bridge-building efforts like mine had no place.

As my book, a deeply personal project meant to foster connection, entered the world, I wasn't just ignored; I was deliberately silenced. The conversations I hoped to spark were off-limits, and my voice was deemed unworthy of the moment. Production meetings for a TV adaptation of my work proved no different. I had network executives moved to tears, inspired by my message, only to receive calls explaining that their hands were tied. Black, indigenous, and people of color (BIPOC) mandates meant opportunities were reserved for women of color, leaving no room for someone who looked like me, regardless of the story, the impact, or the fact that I come from one of the most historically persecuted groups. My voice, my contribution, my very presence in the progressive pantheon was reduced to a black square of solidarity and nothing more.

And then came 2021, when everything shifted. It was as if a lightbulb suddenly flickered on. AOC's voice had become a broken record, bouncing between defunding the police and defunding the Iron Dome.

But it wasn't until I saw what was happening in Israel that I truly woke up. Thousands of rockets—yes, 3,000—fired from Hamas, an internationally recognized terrorist organization in Gaza, rained down on densely populated civilian areas in Israel. An unimaginable situation was unfolding in real time.

What struck me even more was what I saw happening online in the West: race conflation. The BIPOC community was linking the history of race in the United States to geopolitical issues that had, and have, absolutely nothing to do with race.

It all crescendoed in 2023, when those who remained in my corner were mostly fellow members of the tribe and a handful of soul sisters for whom I am eternally grateful. The shift began on October 8th, when I transitioned my content into bipartisan education focused on antisemitism, the hostages, and the safety and security of the State of Israel. What followed was staggering, like digital Ozempic, losing thousands of followers each week. *It's been a chronic slow bleed.*

At first, I was shocked by the sheer scale of the exodus. But then it hit me: this wasn't random. It was a direct reflection of what we, as a culture, had been quietly cosigning for decades: the exploitation of the progressive left's obsession with oppression, where narratives of victimhood often seem to eclipse the nuance of truth.

As a classic liberal and a registered Democrat, this realization cut deeply. I no longer recognize the party I once aligned with; the left officially left me speechless.

Now, as I reflect from the vantage point of a few years later, that New Year's Eve dinner feels like a snapshot of a world I barely recognize. It's not just the upheaval of global events that casts a shadow over that memory; it's the personal betrayals that cut deeper than I ever imagined. Half of the women I welcomed into my home that New Year's Eve, the ones who toasted to friendship and celebrated the future, would no longer sit at my table—not because of a fallling-out. Ex-friends unfollowed, blocked, gossiped, and abandoned me at our shared virtual table. With nothing else changing except for me being even more openly Jewish online, it's not hard for me to imagine that this was the reason.

Over time, I watched curiosity disappear—questions evaporated, conversations thinned, and truth became harder to reach—and what struck me was a kind of social contagion of groupthink taking hold. The silence was deafening, and in it, a reality I could no longer look away from revealed itself: Jewish stories—our voices—didn't matter. Those I believed would stand beside me through thick and thin did not. It wasn't only the absence of support that cut so deeply; it was the presence of something darker—indifference, ignorance, discomfort, and, perhaps worst of all, a willful dismissal.

That dinner, with its glowing candles, heartfelt gifts, and shared laughter, once embodied everything I cherished: connection, joy, and the beauty of creatives coming together to celebrate life. Now, as I write this, it feels like a bittersweet relic from a simpler time, one that felt unchallenged and infantile. Those chairs would now sit empty; over half the table would remain unoccupied.

If this journey has taught me anything, it's that those chairs aren't always reserved for your friends—you will have ghosts at your table, too. I don't say this to romanticize the pain or to indulge in some burdened psychological fantasy. It's merely the most realistic conclusion I've come to.

Some chairs are saved for the uncomfortable truths we'd rather avoid, forcing us to sit with the complexity of relationships, identity, and the shifting terrain of what we believe to be true.

This isn't just a reflection on loss; it's an acknowledgment of growth, the kind that comes when the table shrinks, and the light from the candles burns so much brighter for those who remain.

POST-PARTY: OCTOBER 21st, 2023 AT 2:37 PM

It was a slow Saturday morning, the kind where stillness stretches into the afternoon and the air hints at a changing season. The house was cool, though not quite cold enough to justify turning on the heat. A sweatshirt and a linen blanket did the job. Coffee in hand, I sank deeper into the couch, scrolling through the news, when my phone dinged.

Without thinking, I breathed, *"What the hell."*

Those three words are my baseline these days. I clicked the link that had been sent—mouth open, watching the video.

What unfolded on the screen wasn't just unsettling.

It was a post from my friend—let's call her *Ms. Manifestation Vibration Awakening Ascension Soulwork Cosmic Journey* (you get the point). A spiritual wellness guru with hundreds of thousands of followers. A woman whose business was built on sacred journeys and soft-lit affirmations suddenly had a new offering: a viral clip of the Neturei Karta condemning Israel for defending itself against Hamas.

The Neturei Karta are a fundamentalist wing of the Haredi Jews.[40] The ADL describes them as an ultra-Orthodox, anti-Zionist group that "regularly aligned with international antisemites, Islamic extremists, and groups that advocate violence against Israel."

Translation: they've stood shoulder to shoulder with Holocaust deniers,[41] cozied up to regimes that dream of erasing Israel, and even attended the infamous "Holocaust Review" conference in Iran, nodding along with the worst revisionists of modern history.

And this—not a breathwork tutorial, not an "abundance mindset" meditation—was what my friend chose to amplify.

Sharing a post from this group is like hiring the leader of the Heaven's Gate cult to star in a Nike campaign. You don't elevate fringe extremists and pretend they speak for an entire community. This war is being waged by people who don't even realize they've been recruited to wear the other side's uniform.

THE DANGEROUS GAME OF LANGUAGE: WHEN "ZIONIST" MEANS "JEW"

Words shape reality. They tell us who is worthy of sympathy and who is not. Who belongs and who does not. Who deserves protection and who can be discarded.

And today, one word is being twisted into a weapon.

Whenever you hear the word "Zionist" used as a slur, replace it with "Jew." Because that's what it means. The pejorative use of Zionist is not just casual criticism—it is a calculated, sinister technique with roots in Soviet disinformation and Nazi propaganda. It's a rebranding of the world's oldest hatred, repackaged for the digital age.

Now those same sentiments flood social media. The vilification of Zionism is often just antisemitism with better PR.

Take influencer/grifter @ihartericka, Ericka Hart. After the 2025 Academy Awards, Hart posted a video celebrating *No Other Land* winning an Oscar. But then she received messages from some Palestinian followers, warning her that this was NOT a win. She posted on Instagram on March 3rd, 2025:

> I was super excited when *No Other Land* won the Oscar last night. Oh, right, right, right. A few Palestinian folks messaged me and were like: This is not a win. Like we don't want to win an award in a Zionist space.[42]

Now, let's do the substitution test: "A few Palestinian folks messaged me and were like: This is not a win. Like we don't want to win an award in a Jewish space."

Let that sink in.

In 2025, the same rhetoric that fueled Hitler's speeches—the same language that justified centuries of Jewish exclusion and genocide—is now effortlessly parroted by the very people Hitler would have persecuted.

This is the great irony of modern activism: people fighting oppression while regurgitating the playbook of history's most infamous oppressors.

Language Matters. Precision Matters.

When people say they are against Zionism, what they often mean is that they are against Jewish people having self-determination. They mean Israel should not exist. They mean Jewish spaces are illegitimate.[43] Would they ever say the same about any other indigenous group fighting for their homeland? Would they argue that Tibetans don't deserve Tibet? That Native Americans should have no sovereignty?

No. But for Jews, the rules are different. Always.

So the next time you hear someone use Zionist like a slur, replace it with Jew. See how it sits in your stomach. See how quickly the mask slips.

The American Jewish Committee defines Zionism as a political movement that began in the late nineteenth century, advocating for the reestablishment of a Jewish state in the Jewish ancestral homeland. As a sovereign nation, Israel has the right to self-determine and combat aggressive threats.[44]

On the Rosenheck side of my family, my ancestors were at the forefront of Zionism in both Austria and Nazareth, one of the largest Arab cities in northern Israel now.

It's important to note that the majority of the Jewish community takes pride in being Zionists, while also supporting the Palestinian people's right to statehood. The Pew Research Center study "Jewish Americans in 2020" found that eight out of ten American Jews care and embody Israel as an essential or an important part of what being Jewish means to them."[45]

Advocacy for one does not negate the other.

Anti-Zionism, as the name suggests, opposes the idea of a Jewish state in Israel.[46]

More and more often, the progressive left have been brainwashed to take it upon themselves to dictate what Zionism means to Jews.

To anyone tempted to look at the events of October 7th and say "Aren't there two sides?": Please reread chapter 1 of this book, and consider the heinous acts done to Jewish bodies, Jewish homes, and Jewish wombs.

The line is clear: good versus evil. The stakes couldn't be higher, and the survival of the democratic health of the West, of everything that anchors freedom, justice, and civilization itself, depends on choosing the side that protects us all.

My friends were swept up in false narratives that revise history, and demonize and delegitimize the Jewish community.

It is jarring and surreal to witness the kind of content that reduces Jews to a caricature of ourselves. The Neturei Karta video that unsettled and infuriated me on that Saturday morning was not only deeply misleading, it was posted by someone I respected.

I began drafting a text to "Ms. Guru." I chose my words carefully, mindful of how fragile a moment like this could be. My goal was simple: wave the flag of reflection, and encourage her to pause and be the energy that had been the cornerstone of her brand.

I started the message out:

> Hello, friend. I come to you in peace. I have spent the last 9 days or so making sure loved ones are safe and alive in Israel. It is heartbreaking to watch, and I personally do not know any sane human who wants any of this. My girlfriend, who follows and loves you, sent me the recent video you shared from the "Neturei Karta."
>
> This is a fringe religious group of Haredi Jews currently being tokenized on social media to represent the Jewish majority, which they absolutely do not. The Neturei Karta leaders in the past have had connections to Hezbollah officials, participate in a range of anti-Israel programs, and claim that anti-Zionism is not antisemitism, which stems from Soviet Union propaganda. Anti-Zionism is very much antisemitism.
>
> Al Jazeera [the source of the clip] is a news organization backed by Qatar and funded by Iran, which also funds Hamas (and allows their headquarters in Doha along with Al-Qaeda) and gives a platform to terrorist organizations. This media network that you are using as a source should be approached with

> great caution. Al Jazeera has denied the Holocaust in the past and perpetuates content that harms Jews, Israel, and Western values.
>
> I just wanted to provide context regarding the video shared on your Instagram feed. It hurts my heart as a Jewish woman, and I am here to share resources or have a conversation if you're curious. I am sending nothing but love to you always.

Ms. Guru replied, "Thank you, Alyssa. I appreciate you too. I look forward to listening."

We texted back and forth, and then I called her. Over the course of a draining, three-hour phone call, she revealed that she's neither Jewish, Palestinian, Israeli, nor Arab—yet spoke with the confidence of a self-appointed authority on one of the most volatile and emotionally charged geopolitical issues of our time.

And then came the cosmic asteroid: she casually dropped that she had previously been a member of the Nation of Islam, Louis Farrakhan's religious organization—whose leadership has a well-documented and notorious history for its antisemitic rhetoric and teachings on Black nationalism.[47] There was nothing casual about that admission. For me, it reframed the unease I'd already been feeling—especially after seeing her on social media after October 7th wearing a shayla, when it hadn't been part of her usual style.

I make no claim about her current beliefs—only how that disclosure shaped my understanding of the exchange.

Our conversation spun in circles.

Farrakhan's antisemitism is no secret. As a leader of the Nation of Islam, he has a long, documented history of incendiary rhetoric.[48] In his own words, he has referred to Jews as "termites," described the "satanic Jew," called Hitler a "very great man," and advances the broader claim that Judaism itself is one grand deception.[49]

All of these thoughts swirled in my mind as I continued to have a conversation with her on the phone.

And the *pièce de résistance*?

"I will always stand on the side of the oppressed," she said.

The *High Vibes* landed like a throat punch.

Later that day, as I was still processing our conversation, I followed up, trying to swallow what just happened, with:

> I appreciate you. Here's the link: The History and Ethics of the Israel-Palestine Conflict with Dr. Benny Morris on Conversations with Coleman Hughes.[50]

Then came the emoji parade: *insert brown prayer hands, insert red rose, insert white dove, insert red heart.*

All the feel-good symbols of empty allyship. Nice words, zero action.

Insert the she unfollowed me emoji.

Insert the double-standard emoji.

Insert the fire breathing dragon emoji.

Insert where are those emojis when you need them?

The irony was impossible to miss. It was as if the complexity of a cause could be flattened into a slogan—a form of virtue signaling that, to me, seemed weaponized and blind to the harm it could perpetuate.

I soon realized we were operating from very different understandings of the word "oppression."

How did we get here?

The language of civil rights—rightfully earned through the suffering and perseverance of Black Americans—has, over time, been appropriated and repurposed by Yasser Arafat's Palestinian movement and amplified through the broader machinery of political Islam.

In the article "Why HBCUs Are Key to Fighting Antisemitism,"[51] Dana W. White argues that antisemitism within Historically Black Colleges and Universities (HBCUs) is rooted in Louis Farrakhan's rhetoric.

Farrakhan and the Nation of Islam targeted elite Black students at prestigious HBCUs like Howard, Hampton, Morehouse, and Spelman, where he spread antisemitism, blaming Jews for the transatlantic slave trade and accusing Jews of controlling the economy, government, and media.[52]

Black students were drawn to the ideologies promoted by factions of the Black Panthers, who depicted Jews as capitalist oppressors of Black communities.

White looks to a 1994 speech at Howard University given by Khalid Abdul Muhammad of the Nation of Islam[53] as overt evidence of antisemitic rhetoric found at HBCUs. A law school student named Malik Zulu Shabazz led the audience in a call and response:

"Who caught and killed Nat Turner?" he shouted.

"Jews," some in the crowd responded.

"Who was it that controls the Federal Reserve?"

"Jews."

The controversy surrounding this event led to the resignation of Howard's president.

HBCUs were not always marked by such sentiments. White notes:

> In the 1980s, HBCUs were havens for black excellence, but they became breeding grounds for revenge history or alternative narratives. Inside the classroom, students learned about the outstanding achievements of blacks across multiple disciplines: the sciences, medicine, politics, and economics—accomplishments that had been left out of their public-school textbooks.

White highlights the contrast in ideologies between her parents' generation and her brother's generation. While her parents had a positive view of the Jewish community, shaped by a shared sense of purpose, working together to dismantle Jim Crow and other forms of discrimination, her brother was influenced by college campus culture and developed a distinctly negative opinion of Jews.

White writes, "Without personal, academic, or social connections to Jews, my brother and his peers saw [Jews] as indistinguishable from whites, making them more receptive to Farrakhan's empowerment message and antisemitic rhetoric."

She warns that these ideas have now spread across our top college campuses and led to normalizing both antisemitism and anti-Israel propaganda.

> Many people know that the abolition of slavery and the civil rights movement were Christian-led efforts, but their inspiration was as Jewish as a Passover seder. Both movements drew on the stories and principles of the Hebrew scriptures. Jewish principles of justice, equality, and humanity have been infused in every social movement in this country. It is time to celebrate and remember more of these unsung heroes.

Anti-Jewish and anti-Israel ideas have infiltrated most US college campuses, providing fertile ground for BDS to take root and normalize antisemitism and anti-Israel propaganda across both predominantly Black and white institutions. Social media acts as a high-speed booster, accelerating the spread of these narratives until they resurface in classrooms, protests, and the social media feeds of those who claim to stand against oppression—while parroting civil rights rhetoric.

The antidote? A critical reckoning within the Black community to unlearn the false narratives that cast Jews as oppressors. Real awareness demands more than rhetoric. It requires intellectual honesty and a commitment to factual education. Integrating more Jewish professors into university faculties, reestablishing strong Jewish-Black partnerships at HBCUs, and fostering open, historically grounded dialogue are essential steps forward.

Know your history. Because without it, you risk becoming a mouthpiece for someone else's oppressive agenda.

MALCOLM OR MARTIN'S VISION FOR AMERICA?

We are living amid competing visions for our country. Malcolm X, an eighth-grade dropout and former Nation of Islam leader, promoted Black supremacy and a divisive worldview rooted in separatism, justifying violence as a means to an end. His vision left little room for hope or unity, portraying Black people as perpetually oppressed, disconnected, and supreme over their white counterparts.

In stark contrast, Dr. Martin Luther King Jr., who earned his PhD from Boston University, championed a radical, nonviolent approach to change. He believed in integration, reconciliation, cultural healing, and a future where Black and white Americans could live as equals through courage, compassion, and civil disobedience. King's support for Israel stemmed from this worldview—he saw Zionism as part of the broader fight for justice and human rights, paralleling the struggle for Black freedom.

Both men stirred America's conscience and paid the ultimate price for their convictions. Malcolm X was assassinated in 1965 at the Audubon Ballroom in New York City; three years later, Martin Luther King Jr. was killed on the balcony of the Lorraine Motel in Memphis.

Their deaths remind us that the battle for America's soul has always been costly. Today, we must decide which legacy to embrace—the fractured path of division or the difficult, hopeful road toward unity, peace, and justice.

FALSE EQUIVALENCIES

The suffering Black Americans endured under slavery has been falsely equated with the situation of Palestinians in present-day Gaza. This comparison distorts history and reality. A new form of antisemitism is emerging from the BDS-infiltrated progressive left, Palestinians, and their supporters, who promote what they call "resistance"—but it is a false resistance built on misinformation.

One of the most revealing examples of this psychological manipulation within the BDS apparatus is a USCPR (US Campaign for Palestinian Rights) training toolkit—just one of thousands—designed to "organize your people." This phrase, taken straight from their playbook, exposes a dangerous strategy: targeted indoctrination disguised as grassroots activism. It's like a predator luring a child with candy, except the bait here is language around empathy, oppression, and justice, carefully used to manipulate communities that would actually face brutal persecution or worse under the very regimes they're being conditioned to support.

You can see for yourself in the Google Doc, if it's still available.

The groups BDS exploits include:

> Queer communities, Drag Queens for Palestine, Disabled communities, Indigenous communities, Black communities, Asian communities, Latinx communities, Feminists, Labor movements and unions, Social workers, Non-profit workers, Civil and human rights advocates, Local government workers, Climate justice organizers, Immigration justice organizers, Philanthropy funders, Faith communities, Journalists, Doctors and healthcare workers, Artists, musicians, and writers, Children and families, Educators for 4th-7th graders, Small business owners.

Every single one of these groups would face severe persecution, imprisonment, or execution in Gaza. And yet, through an unprecedented campaign of psychological warfare, they are being groomed to serve as foot soldiers for a Palestinian ideology that would erase them the moment they outlive their usefulness. This is not solidarity—it is weaponized empathy, turning the most vulnerable into unwitting accomplices to their own erasure, as happened during the Arab Spring and the Weimar Republic, where authoritarian regimes routinely exploited liberal and progressive movements to gain power—only to silence, imprison, or eliminate them once that power was secured.

The new form of antisemitism is anti-Zionism. Its purpose is to divide and isolate Jews from their indigenous land of Israel. This is not just a distortion of history, it's flat-out wrong. The civil rights movement in the United States was founded on shared struggles for justice, equality, and freedom. Black and Jewish communities stood together, both fighting against systemic oppression and persecution.

According to recent Pew Research Center data, approximately one in five Black Americans are first- or second-generation immigrants, meaning they or their parents were born outside the United States and have no direct ancestral connection to American slavery.[54] This diversity within the Black American population challenges the binary narratives often wielded in the name of social justice.

Historian Gil Troy explains:

> The Palestinian cause has gained a seat in the progressive sectarian tent by piggybacking off the historical experience of American Blacks. Especially since 2020, Palestine has become thoroughly incorporated into Black Lives Matter sloganeering and visual aesthetics. As a result, an Arab nationalist movement fighting a battle 6,000 miles away from America's Atlantic coast has become a central component of America's "anti-racist struggle," regardless of its lack of even the slightest connection to the historical reality of race-based discrimination in America, or to the values of the American civil rights movement.[55]

Plenty of well-intentioned, left-leaning people are unwittingly becoming vocal proponents of this narrative. Like Ms. Guru, who weaponized this borrowed framework to tokenize a fringe minority within the Jewish community, amplifying their voices to fit an agenda while ignoring the second largest massacre of Jewish lives since the Holocaust just days prior.

In 2020, the unspoken mandate was clear: sit down, shut up, listen, learn, and hold yourself accountable. Had I engaged in similar behavior or dared to tokenize a member of the Black community to serve my own narrative, then I would have faced swift and severe consequences. And if someone had privately called me in, I would have done exactly that, striving to understand and repair any harm caused.

However, when I called Ms. Guru in, asking her to remove disinformation and reflect on the impact of her actions—actions that perpetuated harm against my community—her response was dismissive. Her commitment to her narrative left no room for dialogue, accountability, or the ability to see the humans behind the headlines. And I felt like I still was expected to apologize for my "whiteness."

Instead of listening, she reduced my community, Jews in Israel and the diaspora (outside of Israel), to a reductive binary: oppressor. It was a framework that allowed her to project a geopolitical conflict onto a righteous stage where she was both judge and jury.

What I encountered didn't feel like a genuine commitment to justice. It was a façade, a polished veneer of moral high ground that appeared to crumble under the weight of its own obsession with oppression. It struck me as a blatant disregard for the very people she claimed to champion, the Israelis brutally massacred, broken pelvises, and the innocent Gazans living under a terrorist regime.

This wasn't progress.

This wasn't justice.

This wasn't human.

This was an obsession—a toxic fixation that divides and distorts. This new mind virus of our time trades genuine empathy for hollow virtue signaling and sacrifices truth on the power-grabbing altar of a self-serving narrative.

But we don't have to be trapped in a framework that fractures and misleads.

There's a better way, a way to pace ourselves.

P.A.C.E.

A REFLECTIVE + INTERACTIVE DISCUSSION GUIDE FOR BOOK CLUBS

Breaking Free from the Obsession with Oppression

P PAUSE

Reflecting Before Reacting

Think about a time when you reacted impulsively to a situation related to power, oppression, or identity. What emotions—fear, anger, frustration—drove your response? How might pausing in that moment have shifted your perspective or your actions?

Group Discussion Questions

- When you hear the terms "oppressor" or "oppressed," who do you put into those categories? Where did you first learn this?
- How does social media culture (quick takes, viral rage) shape how you respond to complex issues? Are you limiting your critical thinking around topics on identity?
- What strategies could you use to cultivate a practice of pausing before reacting, especially when the topic feels personal or involves high stakes?
- How does pausing allow space for both empathy and critical thinking?

Activity

Write down a personal example of a time you paused and saw a situation differently than you initially would have in a binary framework. Share and discuss how you would approach that situation differently now after reading this chapter.

A ANALYZE

Group Discussion: Who Benefits from Oversimplified Narratives?

The narratives we consume often frame the world as a simple battle between the powerful and the powerless. Who benefits from this framing? What voices, histories, and complexities are erased when we accept these dichotomies at face value? Are there foreign bad actors driving these narratives creating organized conflict in the West?

Group Discussion Questions

- When have you noticed a situation or conflict being framed in purely black-and-white terms? What context or nuance was left out?
- Who do you think benefits from the oppressor/oppressed binary? Are these narratives driven by ideology, financial incentives, BDS influences, or all of the above?
- How does the media you consume shape your own perceptions of power, justice, and morality?
- What new media outlets would you be open to consuming to soften any sharp edges with an alternative perspective?
- What false narratives around Israel, Zionism, and Jewish identity have you been exposed to, and how have those been shaped by these binary frameworks?
- How does learning about Black–Jewish alliances in the civil rights era shift your understanding of solidarity?

C CONTEMPLATE

To break free from the obsession with oppression, we must explore the histories, connections, and complexities often ignored. Let's dive into real histories that defy the oppressor/oppressed script.

Suggested Reading List

- Bari Weiss, *How to Fight Anti-Semitism*, on ideological oversimplification.[56]
- Douglas Murray, *The Madness of Crowds: Gender, Race and Identity*, on how binary thinking shapes Western discourse.[57]
- David Baddiel, *Jews Don't Count*, about the failure of identity politics.[58]
- Dr. Benny Morris, 1948: *A History of the First Arab-Israeli War.*[59]
- Sam Harris, "Why Don't I Criticize Israel?" on the moral complexity of Israel and the West.[60]
- *Shared Dreams: Martin Luther King and the Jewish Community*, by Rabbi Marc Schneier.[61]

E ENGAGE

From Reflection to Action

What does it look like to engage meaningfully with difficult issues—not from a place of ideological rigidity, but from informed conviction? True engagement requires humility, curiosity, and the courage to challenge both ourselves and the mainstream cultural climate.

Group Discussion Questions

- When engaging in conversations about complex topics (like Israel, race, or power), do you find yourself listening to understand, or preparing to defend your position?
- What techniques help you ask better questions that open up dialogue rather than shut it down?
- How do you vet sources before sharing them?
- Have you ever shared something you later realized was misleading?
- Where are you investing your time, money, and attention? Are you reinforcing the binary narratives you want to resist, or supporting more nuanced conversations and solutions?

- What is one narrative you believed for years that you now see differently?
- How can you become a better steward of your own intellectual freedom, and help others do the same?

Suggested Actions

- Follow independent journalists, historians, and analysts who prioritize context and nuance over ideology, even if you don't always agree with them.
- Support organizations that foster interfaith dialogue, historical literacy, and media accountability.
- Commit to being the person in your community who asks, "What's the full story here?" "Who's behind the story?" "Who's funding the story?" and "What's the agenda?"

CHAPTER 4

JEWS ARE NOT WHITE

I was Jewish HGTV.

My content was light, focused on beauty and design. A celebration of color, texture, trends, and the small joys that make a house a home.

I miss being light.

Back then, I shared light through my work, hoping to remind the viewer on the other side of the screen of the light within themselves. It felt effortless, a simple but meaningful way to connect. My community was diverse, spanning every walk of life and every side of the political aisle. I was the middle ground, a place where differences didn't divide.

I'm still the center. But now, it's a different kind of center, one where my responsibility has shifted. My focus remains on light, but now it's about what it means to be the light in the middle of a storm.

Every Sunday, what was once a space for sharing my latest magazine feature is transformed into something heavier. My platform has become a place to share underreported antisemitic events—not because my community is ignoring these stories, far from it, but because legacy media won't touch them. The omissions are glaring, the silence deafening, and the burden of truth-telling lands on voices like mine. I try to be mindful knowing that our collective attention span, and appetite, for antisemitism has been exhausted. But honestly, no shit.

I avoid jarring visuals and ragey rhetoric (even as I feel the pull of Lauryn Hill's Ready or Not, "Here I come, I'm going to find you" as my battle cry). Instead, I choose a gentler approach. I pair calming videos with soothing music, inviting people in with a sense of ease. It is my responsibility as a Jewish woman to carry a mindful light.

Over the last ten days of penning this chapter, the list continues to grow like a fire surging across the world:

- London, United Kingdom: A Jewish girl was brutally attacked by a grown man with a glass bottle.[62]
- Canada: A video game simulating the October 7th atrocities is available to Canadian gamers on Steam, trivializing terror and violence against Jews.[63]
- United States: Jewish and Israeli Americans report significant discrimination in job application processes, with employer biases increasingly evident.[64]
- Melbourne, Australia: A synagogue was firebombed, FIREBOMBED, while Jewish members were inside, a horrifying act.[65]
- Palermo, California: Two kindergarten boys were shot at a Christian school as an act of "revenge" for an alleged Gaza "genocide"—an accusation that defies both logic with the Gazan population growth and legal definitions.[66]
- Los Angeles, California: At UCLA, a student government official created a "Zionist no-hire list," openly discriminating against Jewish applicants.[67]
- Charlotte, North Carolina: Swastikas and slurs were spray-painted on a Jewish family's home, a desecration meant to intimidate and isolate.[68]
- East Greenwich, Rhode Island: Antisemitic graffiti was found in a high school boys' bathroom, signaling the reach of this hatred into everyday spaces.[69]

- Memphis, Tennessee: An Israeli locksmith was murdered after being lured out on a job, a heinous act targeting him for his nationality.[70]
- Brooklyn, New York: Masked protestors terrorized Jewish neighborhoods, screaming "From the river to the sea," a call to erase the Jewish state.[71]
- Greenwich, Connecticut: An elementary-school child was physically attacked at a party for being Jewish.[72]
- Cambridgeshire, United Kingdom: Jewish students received a swastika in the mail. UK police labeled it a non-hate crime.[73]
- Hoboken, New Jersey: The city council held a flag-raising ceremony for Palestine. A reminder: Palestine is not a recognized country, yet its flag was given a platform over Jewish security concerns.[74]
- Abu Dhabi, United Arab Emirates: A Chabad emissary, Rabbi Kogan, was kidnapped and murdered for being Jewish and strengthening Arab and Israeli relations.[75]
- Montreal, Canada: More than 50,000 Quebec students went on strike "for Gaza," calling for intifada and a "final solution," a term chillingly reminiscent of Nazi rhetoric.[76]

Jews are often miscategorized as white, a misrepresentation that erases both our history and present-day reality. Vanderbilt professor and author Michael Eric Dyson, for instance, claims that Jews have "white eligibility," a label imposed by someone who is neither Jewish nor Israeli, yet feels entitled to conflate the Jewish experience with "white privilege" and only see us through the lens of race:

> The relation of African Americans to Jews cannot be divorced from the pervasive glow and allure and privilege of whiteness. The fact that most Jews are white-eligible and African Americans are white-excluded creates tensions between African Americans and many Jews that have less to do with the cultural

> conflicts between the groups than with the meaning of Blackness and whiteness in America.[77]

This is not only intellectually lazy, especially coming from a professor from the Harvard of the South, but it is inaccurate. Imagine if the roles were reversed—if I attempted to define his lived reality. It wouldn't happen.

Voices like Dyson's fail to grasp the Jewish experience precisely because they refuse to exercise the necessary empathy required of this moment in history, to understand a group facing relentless threats—not as anomalies, but as an ongoing reality.

Imagine a "good day" where the most you endure is a swastika sprayed on a car or house, or the person checking you out at Nordstrom wears a keffiyeh, or the flight attendant wears a pin supporting "Palestine." That's what it means to exist in a world where every moment is a reminder of the hate that simmers beneath the surface.

But on a bad day—and I mean a truly bad day—the horrors are much worse. Innocent girls are gang-raped because they are Jewish. Women are beaten and bruised for simply wearing Star of David earrings. Little boys endure abduction attempts on their way to synagogue. Molotov cocktails are thrown at synagogues, or they're lit on fire. These are not isolated incidents. This is the terrifying reality of being Jewish in a world where violence against you is not a distant threat—it is daily. And sometimes, it's a terrible, relentless week.

Jews are not white. Let's talk about it.

WHITE GIRL BOOK

It was February 15th, 2021. I had just returned to the house from dinner, still wearing my coat when I decided to make the call. This was not a casual check-in. It was a long, overdue conversation that neither of us wanted to have, and one that had been simmering for months.

My film crew and I had been stood up by this individual, and the sting of that moment still lingers. It wasn't just a missed opportunity—it was a punch in the gut. The production team lost not only a job but also their paychecks. My sizzle reel, a key piece for a new show concept tied to my recently released book, was left to die. This was a dream—a big one—and I buried it.

I had landed a production deal, poured countless hours into developing the show alongside my co-executive producer, the cast, the team. The dreams of so many people were riding on it. Standing someone up like this wasn't just a bad business move; it was a betrayal against someone's creative family. And mind you, this wasn't just any moment. It was at the very beginning of the reopening after COVID. Creatives, desperate for work after months of uncertainty, were struggling to find opportunities. Jobs were scarce, and every single chance meant everything.

So, you can imagine the weight of what was lost that day.

I started the call at my kitchen island, pacing back and forth as I laid the groundwork, my voice measured and kind. Eventually, I settled into my office, but the tension hung over my desk like a cloud getting ready to storm.

Her question lingered, daring me to defend myself.

"What have you done for my community?"

Here we go . . .

I took a deep breath.

I told her what I'd done—what I had spent years doing—not for "her" community, but for our Nashville community. Because that's how I see it: a collective of human beings trying to lift one another up, regardless of labels, skin color, or boundaries. But it was clear she saw things differently. "Her" community couldn't have been further from the reality of one in need. No, her community was made up of Ivy League educations, glossy op-eds in *The New York Times*, parents who paid for mortgages and weddings, and cars that came with fully funded gas cards. It was exclusive social clubs, whispered alliances over backyard cocktails on warm southern nights, and nepotism so deeply ingrained that it had already set her up to be the next self-proclaimed Oprah.

This was not a world I knew.

Meanwhile, I had poured my energy into a community where the need was palpable, where young women in under-resourced areas of Nashville needed more than promises and Instagram posts. They needed action. I had worked to provide mentorship, professional skills, and financial literacy, and created a merch line where 100 percent of the proceeds went to trusted nonprofits. I had raised funds and donated to ensure women could access breast reconstructive surgery after cancer, women who wouldn't have been able to afford it otherwise.

And yet, here I was, on the receiving end of her smug dismissal.

So, I matched her question with one of my own. My voice calm, I asked, "What have you done for my community?"

There was a pause.

I could almost hear her recalibrating, the wheels turning as she decided how to respond.

Then she let it slip, casually, as if it were nothing.

"I don't need to apologize. This is just a white girl book."

Ooof.

The words landed heavy, a mixture of dismissal and disdain wrapped in a lazy excuse. For a moment, I sat there, stunned, the air between us growing thicker and the distance traveling farther away from the center.

I took a breath, steadying myself, and then asked, "Have you even read the book you're in?"

Her pause was telling, but her answer was worse.

"No," she said, her voice as casual as if she were commenting on the weather.

Jeesh!

The sheer audacity of her response left me momentarily speechless. She hadn't even bothered to read the work she was so quick to diminish, my book that she had agreed to be part of, the book that carried the weight of a creative community, a palpable humanity, and words that unite rather than divide.

How could someone cast such a sweeping judgment without even engaging with the words, the stories, the people that neighbor her on the page?

This wasn't just arrogance; it was laziness, a willful disregard not just for me but for the work itself.

"Then how," I asked slowly, each word deliberate, "can you claim to know what it is, or isn't?"

Her silence spoke volumes. But it didn't diminish the noise in my head.

Did the pages of my book matter less because of immutable characteristics I couldn't control? Did she not understand, or care, that my story wasn't handed to me? That it wasn't born of connections, but of grit, late nights, and years of unrelenting effort?

I had expected resistance, even criticism, but not this. Not this entitled dismissal from someone who hadn't even taken the time to understand the work, let alone respect it.

"Jews aren't white," I said finally, my voice calm but firm. "And this isn't just about a book. It's about what we choose to see, what we choose to honor. It's about the stories we elevate, and the ones we refuse to silence."

The line was quiet, but the tension was anything but.

I leaned back in my chair, feeling the weight of her presence, a presence amplified by the cultural moment we were living in. It was a time in our country when women like her, regardless of poor behavior, seemed to encounter only green lights, skating past consequences with ease.

But it was in conversations like this, uncomfortable, raw, and inevitable, that I started to truly develop my voice. Speaking up didn't feel like a choice anymore; it had become a necessity. Creativity was still the only universal language I knew, the only way I could build a bridge between worlds. But even that bridge—fragile, beautiful, hard won—would continue to be tested again and again.

I had two show concepts in development at the time. The first was inspired by *The New Southern Style*, the ethos of my debut book, which captured the creative energy of the South through an inclusive, humanizing lens. The show would have been a natural extension of that vision—palpable, intimate, and creatively rich. The book is still going strong years after publication, so I know the idea had staying power.

But something shifted in 2020.

That year, as algorithms shadowed my voice and media gatekeepers amplified only what they labeled "melanated" content, I felt erased. Like so many others with Jewish identities that didn't fit neatly into the binary of oppressor or oppressed, I watched as nuance vanished, and doors quietly closed.

Still, I pressed forward with a second show concept—one I lived and breathed. It centered on helping people design their lives from the inside out, literally building their vision boards into their living spaces. Post-pandemic, we were all asking deeper questions about purpose and sustainability. My show offered practical, uplifting tools for transformation. Everyday people would work with celebrity mentors to cultivate their creative gifts into lasting, meaningful side hustles. It wasn't just aspirational, it was actionable. Dream-building at its finest.

I had a meeting with two major networks and the production team that had recently signed me to their roster. The pitch went beautifully. I moved one of the head buyers to tears. She said she could feel what I was trying to build. I left the call certain this was the moment.

Until it wasn't.

Shortly after we met, the executive producer of my show called. Their voice was quiet and even apologetic.

"Between you and me, Alyssa," they said, "they can't purchase you. They're under a BIPOC purchase mandate. The lead of any new show has to be a Black, Indigenous Person of Color. You don't qualify."

I just sat there.

It was another moment when the air disappeared from the room—when time slows and your body goes cold because you realize that no matter how hard you've worked, no matter how good the idea, it won't matter. Not here. Not now. Everything I had built—my pitch, my passion, my intellectual property—was quietly exiled to a Dropbox graveyard, filed away under *not the right face for this moment.*

Not because it wasn't strong.

Not because I hadn't delivered.

But because I didn't fit the new definition of who was allowed to lead.

I hated life during that time. And honestly? I hated myself. Not in a surface-level, having-a-bad-day kind of way, but in a bone-deep, *what's the point of trying if being yourself isn't enough anymore* kind of way. It was a slow, silent descent into a functioning depression. On the outside, I kept moving. On the inside, I was disappearing.

It cracked everything—my marriage, my home, my work, my sense of self. Suddenly, the foundation I thought I could stand on was rubble. The intensity of it all—the stress, the silence, the slow unraveling—left me too depleted to fight back. Deep down, I think I surrendered. Not in peace, but in quiet defeat. I gave in. I gave up. At the same time.

People still ask if I'd ever revive those concepts. For a while, I clung to that possibility, like revisiting an old love you secretly hope has changed. But the truth? You grow. They don't.

So, I've learned to move forward. To grieve the dream, bury it if I must, and keep building anyway. Creativity always finds another way through. We just have to keep breaking, rebuilding, and listening for the deeper longing underneath it all—the one that wants us to be free.

WHY JEWS ARE NOT WHITE

What does "white" even mean?

Throughout history, Jews were never considered white. Ever. In the seventeenth century, European colonialism and imperialism introduced racial hierarchies to justify the enslavement of indigenous peoples. We have to look beyond our Western lens to understand that race is not a biological fact; it's a social construct that has historically been shaped by those in power to serve their interests.

In America, F. James Davis discusses the "one drop rule," which originated in the South during the era of slavery and was codified into law during the Jim Crow period.[78] Under this rule, anyone with even a single drop of African blood was not considered white. This arbitrary racial categorization had profound consequences for Black Americans, but it also helps us understand the fluidity of racial classifications.[79]

During the Nazi regime, Adolf Hitler promoted the concept of "racial hygiene" and aimed to create an "Aryan race." For Hitler, race was biological, and he deemed Jews, regardless of their physical traits, as a non-white, subhuman race of Levantine origin. While his chillingly false characterization of Jews as "subhuman" is absolutely incorrect, he did get one thing right: our origin story.

All Jews, no matter where we live today, trace our roots back to the Levant—the historic region along the eastern Mediterranean coast. That includes modern-day Israel, Jordan, Lebanon, and Syria. Sometimes, the term stretches a bit to nearby areas, but this core region is where Jewish identity was born and shaped.[80]

So to all the "Keffiyeh Karens" out there insisting that Jews are white, let me be crystal clear: Jews are not, and have never been, considered white. Even Ashkenazi Jews like me—with fair skin, blue eyes, and blonde hair—would have been targeted by the Nazis just like any other Jew. No amount of European features would have spared me.

Jewish Exile

To truly understand why Jews are not white in the diaspora, we must first look at our exile, the force that scattered the Jewish people from Judea across the Middle East, North Africa, and Europe.

Much like the kitchen classic pairing of peanut butter and jelly or cream cheese on an everything bagel, the Jews and exile have an enduring connection throughout history. Here I am, discussing history, a topic that, if you know me (I am laughing), feels almost ironic. I was the one sitting in Sunday and Hebrew school class with glazed-over eyes, lost in a sea of dates and details I couldn't fully grasp. Back then, I didn't understand why it all mattered. But now I see why our history matters more than ever.

This displacement of Jews wasn't just a physical uprooting; it was the start of centuries of Jewish "otherness" in foreign lands. Wherever we went, we lived at the crossroads of two tensions: the pull to assimilate versus the drive to preserve our unique ethno-cultural and religious identities.

The Jewish experience has been shaped by a recurring cycle of exile. We thrive—building, studying, creating communities, and vibrant cultural hubs—and, throughout history, this success has often provoked resentment. Most often, it's simply our existence as a people who embody the belief that all should be free, challenging those in power, that makes us a target. And this is worth fighting for . . . regardless of how many Instagram followers and deals I lose.

This dynamic leads to persecution, enslavement (a far cry from white privilege), and ultimately, exile. Yet here lies the beauty of our story: no matter the circumstances, we return to what we do best: we rebuild, carrying with us an unrelenting light of democracy, fairness, and hope.

CONFLICT CLEO

We all have that one friend who seems to know exactly what's going on before anyone else. I've been blessed with an incredible circle of spiritually connected women in my life—those who call at just the right moment to check in, leave voice memos validating a major life decision (like telling me to leave him), or offer wisdom that feels G-d kissed. And then there's my friend Kyel, whom I affectionately call my "Conflict Cleo." She's the one who calls me first, often predicting global events with eerie precision, especially during this past year and unrelenting months of war—always before the news even breaks.

The prophet Daniel was a bit like that. Daniel did more than hang out with a lion. Think of him as a wartime seer or an exile energy reader.

Daniel was renowned for his prophetic visions, which revealed the cycles of Jewish exile and restoration. He captured it best when he explained:

> "I saw in my vision by night . . . four great beasts . . . The first was like a lion . . . and behold, another beast, a second one, similar to a bear . . . Afterwards I beheld, and there was another, similar to a leopard . . . After that, as I looked on in the night vision, there was a fourth beast—fearsome, dreadful, and very powerful." (Daniel 7:2,7)[81]

In his vision, each "beast" represents one of the four exiles endured by the Jewish people after leaving Canaan. In search of food and shelter during a famine, they journeyed to Egypt (1523–1313 BCE), where they were eventually enslaved by Pharaoh and exiled.

In Daniel's prophecy, the lion symbolizes Babylon (423–372 BCE), marking the first exile. During this time, the Holy Temple was destroyed, and Nebuchadnezzar exiled 10,000 Jews, leaving the remaining to work in the fields.[82]

The bear represents Persia/Media (372–348 BCE), symbolizing the second exile of the Jewish people. During this period, the Jewish people were granted permission to return to Jerusalem and rebuild the Holy Temple.[83]

The leopard symbolizes Greece (371–140 BCE), representing the era when Alexander the Great defeated Persia and brought Israel under Greek rule. During this time, many Jews returned to their ancestral land of Israel to revive their long-held traditions.[84]

However, after Alexander's death, hope for the land faded as a tyrant who opposed the Jews, Antiochus IV, came to power. His reign of oppression continued until a small group of Jews, known as the Maccabees, rose up against Antiochus IV. They successfully defeated him and his armies, restoring hope to the Jewish people. Jews worldwide celebrate this total victory with the holiday of Hanukkah.[85]

The fourth beast, fearsome, dreadful, and powerful, is identified with the Roman Empire. This marked a pivotal era for the Jewish people, beginning in 69 CE, when the community faced aggressive taxes and the Second Holy Temple was reduced to ashes.

I have seen these very ashes with my own eyes, walking along a stone road beneath the City of David where Jesus once roamed, in a private excavation site called The Pilgrimage Road. This period was not only defined by destruction but also by mass murders, crusades, and persecutions, echoing the barbarism of October 7th.

Rabbi Dovie Schochet captures the chilling cycle of centuries-long displacement and persecution of Jewish communities. He describes how, in 1096, the First Crusade annihilated Jewish life across Europe and Israel. By 1144, the first blood libel accused Jews of killing children, igniting a deadly pattern that would echo through generations. During the Third Crusade in 1190, massacres spread through England, followed by the mass public burning of twenty-four cartloads of Talmudic texts in Paris in 1242[86] and the expulsion of Jews from England in 1290.[87] The Spanish Inquisition, beginning in 1478, unleashed one of the darkest persecutions in history. In 1648, Chmielnitzki's forces butchered Jewish populations in Ukraine, marking one of the most traumatic events leading up to the Holocaust.[88] In 1918, more than 60,000 Jews were murdered during the Russian Revolution, scapegoated for economic collapse and political chaos. And in the twentieth century, the Holocaust claimed six million Jewish lives by 1945—an unthinkable culmination of centuries of violence and displacement.[89]

Jews are not white; we are just Jews, connected through our history of exile, faith, and many traditions.

Historically, Europeans equated "whiteness" with Christianity, and this connection has shaped how Jews have been perceived.

In modern America, "whiteness" is a relatively new social construct. Jews have only been loosely associated with it during the twentieth century and, even then, were often considered "white-passing" rather than fully included within the category of "white."[90]

Genetic evidence reveals that Jews descended from the Twelve Tribes of Israel, including Ashkenazi Jews, whose origins trace back to the Levant, near present-day Turkey. While some Jews in America may appear to be "white-passing" due to social constructs,[91] this does not change the fact that our ethnic and cultural roots are far older and far more diverse.[92]

In Israel, this diversity is even more apparent. The Jewish population, which comprises 73.5 percent of the country, is a mosaic of ethnicities and appearances.[93] There are Ashkenazi Jews from Eastern and Western Europe and Russia, Mizrahi Jews from the Middle East and North Africa, and Sephardic Jews whose ancestors lived in Spain and Portugal.[94] (For the record, my cousins are Sephardic and look nothing like me, which reinforces the point that Jews are not white.)

Israel is home to Jews from across the globe, including Jews of Asian descent from India, Central Asia, and China, as well as Sub-Saharan African Jews from Ethiopia, Uganda, and Nigeria. This diverse, multi-ethnic population highlights that Jews, by their very nature, are not "white."

In the end, Jews are defined by our shared ethno-culture dating back more than 3,000-plus years, not by the arbitrary racial categories that have been applied to us over the last 200 years. We are a people shaped by centuries of exile and resilience, and our diversity is one of our most defining features. We are simply Jews, unique and united in our shared heritage, no matter where we come from or what we look like. We are one big family.

Finally, "WHITE" is not a dirty word! Can we stop obsessing over our immutable characteristics? Honestly, I couldn't care less about the color of your skin or eyes—what matters more is whether you're leading with character, kindness, and compassion. (Unless, of course, you're on the hunt for a guy in finance who's 6'5" with blue eyes. In that case, carry on, TikTok).

P.A.C.E.

A REFLECTIVE + INTERACTIVE DISCUSSION GUIDE FOR BOOK CLUBS

Jews Are Jews

P PAUSE

Before diving into conversation, take a quiet moment. When you hear the word "Jew," what image comes to mind? Write down your first thoughts without editing yourself—don't overthink it. Is your mental image tied to a particular look, geography, language, or cultural expression? Where do you think that image comes from—your upbringing, media, personal experience, or something else? Have you even met a Jew?

Book Club Discussion Starter:

Go around the room, each person sharing one word or phrase that came to mind when you picture a Jew. No judgment, just observation. Let's explore together how our collective mental images have been shaped, and whether they reflect the full reality of Jewish diversity or tropes that need to be unlearned.

A ANALYZE

Break into pairs or small groups. Each group chooses a Jewish community to research for 10-15 minutes (this can be done in advance, or live if you're meeting virtually or in person with internet access). Examples:

1. Mizrahi Jews (Middle East and North Africa)
2. Sephardic Jews (Spain, Portugal, and Mediterranean)
3. Ethiopian Jews (Beta Israel, East Africa)
4. Indian Jews (Bene Israel, Cochin Jews)
5. Ashkenazi Jews (Central and Eastern Europe)

Each group is tasked to:

- Find a photo or visual of that community.
- Identify one unique cultural tradition (a food, language, or holiday practice).
- Share how this community's appearance, culture, or experience complicates the "Jews are white" narrative.

Discussion Questions:

- How did learning about these communities shift your understanding of Jewish identity?
- What surprised you the most?
- How have stories of non-European Jews been represented (or erased) in the media you've consumed?

C CONTEMPLATE

Personal Journal Prompt (Share with the Group):

How does the concept of whiteness operate in your own life? How have you seen it applied (accurately or inaccurately) to Jewish people? How does labeling Jews as "white" erase history, complexity, or lived experiences?

Book Club Discussion Starter:

Let's navigate this together: What does it mean when Jews are called "white" in certain contexts—and not white in others? How does this shifting label serve political or ideological agendas? How can we push back on binary thinking and reclaim a more accurate and nuanced understanding of Jewish identity?

E ENGAGE

As a group, brainstorm ways to bring the richness of Jewish diversity into your own spheres, whether that's in your social circles, online presence, professional spaces, speaking events, or even future book club selections. Additionally, when you hear someone flattening Jewish identity into "white" or "privileged," commit to speaking up and offering a broader, fact-based view.

WHITE.

BLONDE.

JEW.

CHAPTER 5

BOTTLED BLONDE

Did you know "natural" blondes are practically unicorns? Seriously, they make up less than 2 percent of the world's population.[95] Fun fact: that's about the same percentage as the global Jewish community. So, I guess that makes me extra magical—or extra judged, depending on the day.

News flash: I'm not a natural blonde.

Shocker, I know.

I was blonde as a kid, but somewhere along the way, my hair forgot its roots, pun intended. Now, every few months, I'm perched in a salon chair, coffee in hand, while my stylist, Chelsea, brings my "blonde ambition" back to life.

Effortless? Ha, not at all.

Let's just say I've been called high maintenance more times than I care to count, but I never miss the chance to fire back with "I'm high performance" as my verbal exclamation point.

Here's the thing about being blonde: it's not just a hair color; it's a full-blown persona. Like it or not, it comes with its own set of assumptions, judgments, and, yes, baggage. Blonde is a stereotype magnet, a contradiction factory. You're either the bombshell or the punchline, desired or dismissed. Smart? Sure, maybe—but only after you've proven it. Twice.

Dumb? Absolutely—if the joke lands. And underestimated? Always. My book agent likes to call that my superpower. At first, I rolled my eyes, but the more I think about it, the more I understand what she means.

Being blonde means living in this weird tension between judgment and admiration. It's like a never-ending dance where you have to let your authenticity shine without letting other people's assumptions box you in. You walk into a room, and the world is already halfway through writing your story before you've had the chance to open your mouth.

Are you the femme fatale or the girl next door? Promiscuous or prudish? Over-sexualized and easy, or demure and untouchable? Wealthy and living in the lap of luxury, or destined for a trailer park in Alabama? "Blondes have more fun" is an unshakable myth. Until you're caught in the corner with a book and glasses, suddenly branded as the exception to the rule. It's like you're expected to fit into every stereotype simultaneously, whether it makes sense or not.

The truth is, being blonde is a lesson in navigating contradictions. People are so busy deciding who you are based on their assumptions that they forget you're an actual person, not a trope.

Some people might find that exhausting. Me? I find it thrilling.

I like to prove them wrong.

Meet the chip on my shoulder—it's been riding shotgun for a while now—belting out a power ballad. And there's nothing more satisfying than flipping the script. When you take control of the narrative, when you surprise people with depth, intelligence, and ambition, it's like watching preconceived notions shatter in slow motion.

You show them they're playing checkers when you're out here playing chess.

Because here's the truth: what they see, or think they see, should never overshadow who you actually are. Navigating that space, owning your story while defying theirs? That's not just a skill. It's a fine art.

That's the real magic trick. And trust me, there's no hair color that can teach you resilience quite like being blonde.

TOXIC TRAITS

If I have a toxic trait, it's called: "I am not checking my emails."

I was at my desk, editing a photography project for a client, when my phone rang. I glanced down: Rea, my creative peer, my fellow author, my machine of a friend who cranks out books like she's got a factory of tiny elves typing for her.

I hit speaker.

"Are you coming to my book club?"

Without knowing the date or details, I immediately said yes. We all have that one friend we pick up for. Rea is one of mine.

"What's the book?" I asked.

"You didn't get my email?"

"Rea," I deadpanned. "I'm not checking them. It's my new personality."

She laughed and then, with way too much enthusiasm, said the book title: "*Pussy.*"

Regret. Instant, full-body regret. What in the Eve Ensler hell did I just agree to? She better not have handheld mirrors ready for us to sit in a circle and sing Kumbaya. None of my personalities can handle that.

The book club was two days away, so off I went, multitasking like a pro—editing photos while listening to *Pussy: A Reclamation*.[96] Surprisingly, it was decent. Regena Thomashauer laid it out: women have a fundamental right to pleasure, and that ecstasy can literally save our lives. Scientifically, she explained how orgasms release nitric oxide from our endothelial lining, which balances hormones and boosts health. She talked about embodiment, intuition, and how we should be experiencing daily orgasms like we're running our own inner pharmacy. Casual.

Between meetings and edits, I absorbed it.

Then, book club night, I rushed in, still mentally tangled in my work, wearing a pink button-up, ripped jeans, and gold Birkenstocks—classic "this is the best I can do today" attire. I hugged Rea, threw my purse down, and made my way downstairs.

First breath of fresh air: this was the first time in months I had been around people not affected by the war. My bandwidth for small talk was at an all-time low, but I wanted the break. I wanted new faces. I wanted community.

The room was cozy—floor pillows surrounding a table loaded with sushi (fitting), snacks, and a ceramic bowl of conversation prompts. I smiled at the women, scanning for a cookie before picking a pillow. A woman in a flowy dress sat beside me, flashing a polite smile. I recognized her. I'd been in her home for Rea's last book launch. She did not recognize me. Fine by me.

Rea passed the conversation bowl to a striking Black woman. She introduced herself, then read the prompt. Her response carried a clear through line—personal power. She spoke of her family's origins in South Africa, weaving history into the present. The discussion began lightly, but soon, it caught the current of culture.

And then it happened.

A woman—a strong, intelligent, beautiful human—made a sweeping generalization.

"Black bodies are less important than white bodies," she said.

A bolt of energy shot through me, electric and undeniable. My body reacted before my mind could catch up. The words spilled out, urgent and unfiltered:

"Do you feel that way in this room? Do you feel that in your day-to-day life, here in Nashville, in our creative community—like right now?"

My pulse pounded. My breath came fast. Heat surged through me—not metaphorically, but physically. I steadied myself. Be calm. Be clear. Make space.

And then I said it.

"If there are any bodies worth less right now, it's Jewish and Israeli bodies—the ones being used as weapons of war. Through rape. Through murder. Through literal abduction. Those are the bodies no one cares about or are speaking about."

The room held its breath.

The conversation bowl was quickly passed to the right in an effort to shift the energy.

Then a self-proclaimed trauma specialist with dreadlocks took the floor. I don't know her credentials, but I do know she was having a full-blown performance moment, pandering to the only Black woman in the room with every buzzword she could find. She spewed "intersectionality," "whiteness," and "oppression" like she was competing in a woke spelling bee.

And then—bam. Another lightning strike. This time, in the form of me clearing my throat.

Annoying? Absolutely. But at this point, I had lost all control over what was coming out of my mouth. I was literally blacking out.

"We need to be careful when we discuss 'whiteness' in society," I interjected, my words inspired by Pamela Paresky, spilling faster than my filter could catch them. "Because historically, that conversation has been very dangerous for the Jewish community. When whiteness is framed as a moral good, Jews are dehumanized. When whiteness is framed as a moral evil, Jews become the ultimate oppressor. Either way—both roads lead to destruction."[97]

I barely paused before pushing forward.

"What you're quoting—Kimberlé Crenshaw, intersectionality—it's contemporary Marxism. Soviet-era propaganda, repackaged.[98] And it's dangerous."

I had no idea if I'd just gotten myself kicked out, but I didn't care and continued.

"The Jewish community is a barometer for society's conscience," I finished, my voice steady, despite the heat rising in my body, beads of sweat forming at my temple. "We need to be mindful of what we say, so we don't repeat history."

I took a breath. The room was silent. And then:

"But hey, at least we all have pussies."

I awkwardly laughed, trying to bring it back home while a bead of sweat rolling down my spine betrayed me.

Someone coughed. Another shifted on their cushion, rethinking every decision that led them to this moment. Trust me, I was right there with them.

My timing? Ooof.

Impact? Unmistakable.

Eventually, the conversation moved on. Mouths moved, words floated, but I couldn't hear anything over the pounding in my chest—my heartbeat lodged somewhere between my throat and my ribs. The bowl continued its ritualistic passing, weaving its way through the room.

And then, it landed in my hands.

I braced myself. Convinced I was about to pull the dreaded "How many times a day do you self-pleasure?" question. And let me tell you—I did not have the stamina for that after what had just come out of my mouth.

Instead, the prompt was about life pivots.

So, I shared.

I shared how I lived a life dictated by fear until I was diagnosed with cancer. How I had spent years chasing arbitrary markers of stability and success through two Fortune 100 companies, believing that achievement would somehow quiet the gnawing anxiety inside me.

I shared how, for a brief moment, we thought the cancer had spread to my lungs—and if it had, I wouldn't be sitting in that room at all.

I shared how I was raised by a degenerate fuck who pissed away the American Dream. How my high school guidance counselor looked me dead in the eye and said I'd make a good stripper because my grades suggested I wasn't good for much else. I shared how, in the aftermath of cancer, I reclaimed my power. Not in boardrooms or paychecks, but in creativity. How I picked up a camera for the first time and, in doing so, discovered parts of myself I never knew existed—my courage.

How that tiny machine, built to capture light, illuminated a path forward I never could have imagined.

And how, from that moment on, I never once looked back.

I watched as some of the women who had written me off moments ago softened. Respect found its way back into the room.

The night ended. I left convinced I would never be invited back. I laughed about it.

Then, I got a text from Rea.

"You were brilliant."

I exhaled. "Hope I didn't offend anyone."

"Absolutely not."

The next day, Rea called.

"Do you know who you were sitting next to?"

"Oh G-d, no."

"Ami McConnell."

I blinked. "Wait. I know Ami, but I don't know know Ami."

Rea laughed. "She used to be VP of Editing at Simon & Schuster. And VP of Editorial at HarperCollins and started its fiction division."

I nearly dropped my phone. "Oh. Cool. So I was a total fire-breathing dragon last night?"

"She loved you," Rea said. "She's a huge fan of your book. Didn't realize she was sitting next to the author of one of her favorite housewarming gifts. And she wants to meet with you. She wants to see how she can bring *White. Blonde. Jew.* to life."

Boom.

Why is this important? Because last year, I was on the cusp of my second book deal. A big one.

And then the war happened.

The previous editor, the one I had jumped through hoops for, reshaping my book from creative nonfiction to a workbook and back again, dropped me like a bad habit.

Before the war, she said I had knocked it out of the park. Weeks later? Suddenly, I didn't have enough "coaching experience." Coaching experience that was never part of the book. Coaching experience that was never asked for in month one, six, or nine of the process. And I *have* coaching experience—with the testimonies to prove it. It wasn't an oversight. It was an excuse. And I saw through it.

Overnight, my inbox, once alive with anticipation and waiting on a green light from the publisher, became a void. My contacts? Scattered. My name? Too dangerous to be attached to.

White.

Zionist.

Colonizer.

Genocidal.

Jew.

All the dirty words of the modern era, slapped onto me without hesitation. No conversation. No questions. Just labels, sharp as knives, meant to cut me out of the narrative entirely.

I stopped writing for six weeks. The first four? A blur of empty ice cream cartons and headlines that made my stomach turn. If I was going to spiral, I might as well do it with pints of Häagen-Dazs in my lap, making sure my loved ones affected by the conflict were alive.

Then I went to Israel.

I touched the pain. The purpose. I stood where the world told me not to stand, looked at the destruction they told me not to see. And somewhere in the rubble, I found the fire again.

I came back ready to write.

I finished my new book proposal in five weeks—something that should have taken nine months. Rea kept me accountable. We sent it to agents.

Most declined.

"Too risky."

"Too much."

"Too controversial."

And, of course, they underestimated me.

But then—one night, one room full of strangers, one unfiltered conversation about the power of the P . . . and suddenly, a door opened.

Ami McConnell had underestimated me too that night, until I opened my mouth.

We went for a walk to discuss my new book title. At one point, she stopped me on the trail at Radnor Lake, and looked at me in the eye.

"I need to apologize, Alyssa."

I raised an eyebrow. "For what?"

"Because I didn't expect you to be who you are. I thought you were just a sweet blonde. But then you spoke."

Turns out, people do that a lot.

Turns out, they've always done that.

But Ami didn't stay there.

She leaned in. She broke through her assumptions. And she listened.

She believed in my voice when others turned away.

When most were afraid to hear what I had to say, she chose to help amplify it.

She helped usher my words into the world with the kind of unwavering faith only someone who truly sees you can offer.

And because she did—you're holding this book in your hands right now.

Not by accident.

Not by chance.

But because truth has a way of finding the light, when just one person dares to hear it.

MESSENGER

During WWII, the Kashariyot[99]—Jewish women, many of them young, the majority of them blonde—became the unseen veins of the resistance, slipping past Nazi suspicion with nothing but their wits and the illusion of innocence. They were couriers, smugglers, messengers of life and death, walking through occupied territories with forged papers and steel nerves.

They carried secret notes tucked into the hems of their skirts, pistols baked into loaves of bread, explosives wrapped in silk scarves. They moved between ghettos, forests, and underground networks, passing weapons to fighters, delivering intelligence to resistance leaders, and whispering warnings that saved lives.

The Nazis didn't see them as a threat. How could they? They were young. They were girls. Their hair was too golden, their smiles too sweet, their presence too familiar to warrant suspicion. Their greatest weapon was the enemy's arrogance. The men at the checkpoints, the soldiers on the trains, the collaborators in the streets—none of them expected the messengers of war to wear ribbons in their hair and carry themselves like schoolgirls.

The Kashariyot used the world's underestimation against it, turning every assumption into an opportunity. They played the role expected of them, then walked straight into danger, their sweet blonde demeanor their most dangerous disguise.

I think about them often. About what it means to be dismissed before you even open your mouth. About how people look at a blonde woman and decide they already know her story. But like the Kashariyot, I've learned that when the world misjudges you, it hands you a kind of power. It gives you room to move in the shadows, to be a conduit of a greater message, to speak when no one expects it, to carry truth across lines no one is watching.

I was a messenger, too. And I kept speaking up.

P.A.C.E.

A REFLECTIVE + INTERACTIVE DISCUSSION GUIDE FOR BOOK CLUBS

Unbottling the Blonde

P PAUSE

Take a moment to reflect on your initial reaction to this chapter.

- What emotions surfaced as you read about the assumptions placed on blondes?
- Did any of the experiences with stereotypes, book club tension, or the urge to speak up resonate with your own life?
- What's a label or stereotype you've had to navigate in your life? How did it shape how you show up in the world today? How can you transmute it into personal power?

Body Check-In/Self-Empowerment Reflection: Close your eyes for a moment and bring your awareness into your body.

- Where do you feel the most powerful in your body right now?
- Is it in your chest when you speak your truth?
- In your hands when you create?
- In your legs when you stand firmly in your values?
- Where in your body do you feel the energy of self-trust and alignment?

Writing Prompt

What does it feel like, in your body, when you know you're standing in your truth—even if your voice shakes?

A ANALYZE

Let's break down some of the core themes.

In this chapter I draw a parallel between being blonde and being Jewish—both identities that come with heavy assumptions, judgments, and outside narratives.

I step into a space of discomfort at the book club, where identity, race, and politics collide.

Discussion Points:

- Do you use humor to disarm tension? Where can you do so more?
- What did my instinctive response in the book club reveal about your values and your relationship to yourself and your truth?
- When have you felt the need to challenge a sweeping statement or assumption in real time?
- What held you back—or what pushed you forward? (And what blonde friend do you want to send this chapter to?)

C CONTEMPLATE

Draw Strength from the Kashariyot

During World War II, a group of young Jewish women known as the Kashariyot risked everything to serve as couriers. They carried weapons, intelligence, and life-saving messages between ghettos and resistance groups. These women moved through cities and across borders—sometimes disguised as Polish peasants, sometimes blending in with non-Jewish communities, always adapting, always aware.

Their power didn't come from physical force. It came from their sharp minds, quick thinking, and unshakable sense of purpose. They understood the dangers they faced, but they moved forward anyway—because truth, survival, and resistance depended on their courage.

That same kind of courage is needed today. It may not look like smuggling messages across enemy lines, but it's present in every moment you choose to speak up when it's easier to stay silent, to ask hard questions when the answers feel uncomfortable, or to stand firm in your values even when you're outnumbered. (Especially when it comes to BDS, which we'll discuss in chapter 10.)

Reflection Prompts

- Where in your life are you being called to step into this kind of bravery, the kind rooted in intellect, clarity, and conviction?
- How might you become a modern-day Kashariyot using your voice, your insight, and your willingness to engage to open minds, build bridges, or disrupt harmful assumptions?
- When you learn about these courageous women, how does it reshape the way you see your own inner strength and potential for impact?

Courage in the Body

- When you're about to step into bravery—what do you feel physically?
- Does your chest tighten and your heart race, or do you feel an inner steadiness, a grounding deep in your center?
- How can you learn to recognize those sensations, not as signs to pull back, but as confirmation you are on the edge of something meaningful—a place where your voice and presence matter most?

E ENGAGE

This chapter isn't just my story—it's a mirror and a call to action. It invites each of us to:

- Engage with the stories we've inherited about others—and the ones we've inherited about ourselves.
- Engage with the bravery it takes to break silence, especially when silence would keep us safe and small.
- Engage with the labels and narratives we've quietly accepted, and decide which ones no longer serve us.

Book Club Activity: The Conversation Bowl

Create a conversation bowl for your group. Write down questions from this chapter—or craft your own—and pass the bowl around. Each person draws a question and answers honestly, without editing themselves to please the room. Invite the kind of brave, unfiltered truth-telling this chapter models, the kind that creates connection through vulnerability and can potentially disrupt old ways of thinking.

Empowerment Prompts: Rewriting Your Labels

- What's one label, imposed by others, by society, or even by yourself, that you're ready to rewrite?
- How will you take the pen back?
- Who would you be without that label, and what truth is waiting underneath it?

You are the author. You are the editor. You are the story.

CHAPTER 6
THE ROOTS OF DISINFORMATION

So, a blonde walks into a terrorist bot farm.

Sounds like the setup for a bad joke, only missing a rabbi and an attorney, right?

The punch line? Thousands of faceless accounts, an avalanche of targeted harassment, and the realization that I had accidentally stepped into something much bigger than myself. I didn't mean to stumble into the dark underbelly of the internet, but there I was.

I set out to write this chapter with a little levity, but the deeper I looked, the less funny it became. And isn't that always the case? Scratch the surface, and what we find is often a mirror to ourselves.

This is the tale of how I walked straight into a terrorist bot farm. There are scenes of intimidation, digital arson, and yes, a call to the FBI. Spoiler alert, I know—but stick with me. Because once you see beyond the screen, you realize that the roots of disinformation always come down to two things: fear and power.

But here's where it gets a little complicated. Stripping away the lies, the manipulation, and the intentional harm, there's still a person behind it all. A human leveraging a platform, growing an audience, and—consciously or not—using the internet as a tool for influence. It made me pause. Because despite the stark divide between truth and propaganda, there's still something fundamentally relatable at play.

And that's what makes disinformation so dangerous. It's not just bots and bad actors—it's real people, convincing themselves and others of an alternate reality.

So, before we dive in, here's to a little honest self-reflection. Because if we're going to talk about disinformation, we owe ourselves that much.

DOCTORING REALITY

It started with a doctor. Safe, right?

Wrong.

We'll call her "Mrs. MD"—a Pakistani-born physician with a massive internet following. Scrolling through her Instagram, I noticed something familiar. She knew, as I did, how perception becomes reality online. Her feed was wrapped in a soft palette of blushes, pinks, and greens. I caught myself admiring her home design transformations, and her before-and-afters. I related to her love of family, her eye for beauty, and her curated creativity. It was disarming—because beneath the aesthetic lay an apparatus of influence capable of reshaping truth itself.

I kept scrolling—and then snapped back to reality. A reality where Mrs. MD makes an "URGENT APPEAL" on behalf of her "colleagues" at Al Helou and Al-Shifa Hospital, a facility that was later exposed as a Hamas command center—where so-called "humanitarian doctors" the media platformed were in fact part of Hamas's military leadership[100] And then there are the photo ops—where Mrs. MD is posed with figures like Bisan Owda,[101] who is allegedly connected to the Popular Front for the Liberation of Palestine (PFLP),[102] an internationally recognized terrorist organization (and who is being pushed in BDS toolkits, which are widely disseminated to millions of impressionable minds). See for yourself here:

On a quiet Saturday morning, Mrs. MD grabbed a viral video and dropped it into her feed. A neatly packaged piece of visual propaganda, engineered to travel faster than the truth ever could.

It was a slow morning for me. The kind where the air still feels soft, your coffee is still hot, and—for a fleeting moment—the world just seems so manageable. In my hands, the internet is still a place for creativity, connection, and truth-seeking.

I'm scrolling, half-distracted, when SLAP—a video stops me cold.

An IDF soldier, in full uniform, seemingly kicking an elderly Muslim woman to the ground.

No context. No explanation. Just a violent, gut-wrenching moment, that bypasses logic and goes straight for the emotional jugular.

A rush of horror. Then doubt. Then something deeper. Something sharper.

Something just doesn't sit right.

For all the complexity, all the nuance, some things are certain. Armies, for better or worse, reflect the societies they serve. And I knew that an Israeli soldier would not, unprovoked, attack a defenseless elderly woman.

The Israeli Defense Forces operate under strict ethical codes, rooted in the dignity and value of human life. *Ruach Tzahal*, which means "Spirit of the IDF," is the ethical code all IDF soldiers follow. There are rules, there are laws governing the use of force. The Ruach Tzahal outlines three fundamental values of the IDF as follows: Defense of the State, its Citizens and Residents; Patriotism and Loyalty to the State; and Human Dignity.[103]

The IDF and its soldiers are obligated to preserve human dignity. All humans are to be valued, regardless of race, creed, nationality, gender, status or role:

From these core values stem the concept of Purity of Arms:

> The IDF serviceman will use force of arms only for the purpose of subduing the enemy to the necessary extent and will limit his use of force so as to prevent unnecessary harm to human life and limb, dignity and property.[104]

The IDF servicemen and women extend these values to soldiers and civilians, with special considerations for the defenseless, whether in wartime, or during routine security operations, or in the absence of combat, or in times of peace. There are consequences for those who violate it.

The IDF even rescues stray dogs in Gaza.

With this in mind, I pause. Rewind. Watch again.

Something still isn't adding up.

Rather than letting outrage hijack my reasoning, I do what any rational person with Wi-Fi, caffeine, and a healthy dose of skepticism would do: I go on a digital scavenger hunt . . . an aggressive excavation of URLs.

Less than ten minutes later, I find it.

The full clip.

The real clip.

The one where that same IDF soldier is leaning against a stone wall when a fully covered woman in a black burka suddenly pulls out a knife and starts stabbing him—relentlessly.

The soldier, caught off guard but much larger than she is, shoves her off, causing her to fall to the ground.

A completely different story than the one Mrs. MD reshared, with the title over the video in her feed screaming: "How Israeli occupation forces treat Palestinian women."

And that's when I saw the line of demarcation.

This is where two sides exist in war—and our choices reveal which side we stand on.

Objective evil was present.

A doctor—a human being whose very profession is devoted to helping and healing—had become an active participant in spreading a video that distorted reality, manufactured outrage, amplified misinformation, and endangered lives.

I took a sip of coffee and I corrected the video in my stories.

And then, I reached out to her privately, giving her the chance to correct her error.

A simple, decent thing. A chance to choose truth over evil.

And that's when things got . . . well, interesting.

Rather than rechecking her source, admitting she might have been wrong and deleting the post, she doubled down.

BOT ARMY

Misinformation by definition is the spread of inaccuracies and falsehoods, and it's common on social media. Just a quick scan on Facebook or X reveals its presence. Then there's the insidious nature of disinformation.[105]

Disinformation is created and shared to deliberately deceive.[106]

Disinformation is much like a virus, infiltrating the mind, replicating with every click, and spreading its toxic agenda, distorting truth and eroding sanity with each passing swipe.[107]

Dr. Sander van der Linden, a social psychologist at the University of Cambridge, shows that even when disinformation is debunked, nearly two-thirds of people continue to believe it or remember it as true,[108] a phenomenon known as the "continued influence effect."[109]

The distribution of an edited video of a man in an IDF uniform kicking an elderly woman is a calculated move in the ongoing war of disinformation (with the part where the woman attempts to stab him conveniently cut out). It's one of many tactics used by BDS and terrorist regimes to isolate, delegitimize, and demonize the state of Israel. By distorting what we see on our screens, they gain the power to control not only who we hate but also what we believe. Whether it's a doctor, living comfortably in America, hiding behind a blush-toned color palette, or a verified user on X monetizing outrage, they are part of an information war.

I messaged Mrs. MD directly, asking to pause and to encourage a peaceful, constructive conversation. She ignored the note—and she made sure I knew it.

There was no conversation. No dialogue.

For sixteen straight hours my inbox, comments, and emails were flooded nonstop—an avalanche of abuse arriving several times a minute. The messages ranged from urgent threats to blunt dehumanization: some told me to "go kill yourself," others invoked violent punishments, and many trafficked in language like "Hell is ready for you, insha'Allah," all designed to erase a person and break them down.

This wasn't ordinary backlash. It was a silencing apparatus, fueled by something inhuman and unlike anything I had seen online before.

And I'm sure it works on most people.

But here we are—with loud words in print.

THE PSYCHOLOGY OF DISINFORMATION

According to a 2018 study published in *Science*,[110] false information spreads quantitatively faster and more widely than the truth. On average, fake news stories reach 1,500 people six times quicker than true stories. Additionally, misinformation is 70 percent more likely to be retweeted. Why? Because we're not just rational creatures, we're emotional beings.

When we encounter misinformation, we don't instinctively pause to analyze; we react. Often with outrage, fear, or shock. Neuroscientific research shows that these emotions activate the amygdala, the brain's emotional processing center, compelling us to share content impulsively. This phenomenon is often referred to as "emotional contagion," where strong emotions spread rapidly through social networks, bypassing critical thought.[111]

That's why fabricated stories like the doctored video I encountered are so powerful. They aren't crafted to inform; they're engineered for virality, designed to make us feel before we think. The psychological pull of misinformation is particularly potent in times of crisis, like war, when our brains are primed for heightened emotional responses.[112]

How Disinformation Spreads: The Predictable Pipeline

As quickly as it spreads, disinformation tends to follow a foreseeable pattern:

Seeding the Narrative. A falsehood is introduced, often by a bad actor or an influencer with a large following. The goal is to create a story that is both emotionally compelling and easily shareable.

Outrage Economy. Legacy media aren't just reporting the news, they're in the business of keeping you hooked. With more outlets shifting to a subscriber-based model, the pressure to retain readers and viewers has never been higher. And what's the best way to do that? Emotional highs and lows. Outrage. Fear. Political heroin. It's not about informing, it's about addiction. Social media platforms work the same way, using algorithms that push the most reactive content to the top of your feed. The result? A constant stream of dopamine hits, designed to keep you engaged, enraged, and subscribed.

Reinforcement Via Echo Chambers. I don't like to argue for the sake of it. But let's be real: most people aren't looking to be challenged. We naturally gravitate toward information that reinforces what we already believe. That's confirmation bias at work. Once disinformation sinks in, it's rarely questioned, and anyone who dares to push back is quickly ignored. Or worse, attacked.

Mainstream Legitimization. When a false claim gains enough traction, it often gets picked up by media outlets, influencers, or political figures, cementing its place in the digital town square.

Here are the real-world consequences of disinformation that extend far beyond the palm of our hand. Watchdog group HonestReporting exposed how mainstream media bias, omissions, and underreporting have fueled rising antisemitism since October 7th. Their analysis revealed a deliberate and disturbing pattern: as the negative coverage of Israel grew, so did the violence against Jews. They stated: "There is a strong correlation between the months that antisemitism spiked and negative coverage of Israel in the media and online during those same months."[113]

Research from CyberWell exposed a chilling reality from October 7th: antisemitic content and calls for violence against Jews and Israelis skyrocketed, with an 81 percent spike on X (formerly Twitter) and a staggering 193 percent surge on Facebook in just one week.[114]

Additionally, a case study from the Atlantic Council's Digital Forensic Research Lab found that misinformation about the Israel-Gaza war spiked by over 1,300 percent in the first 48 hours.[115]

HonestReporting also exposed how the media framed the assassination of Hamas leader Ismail Haniyeh in Tehran. Outlets like *Reuters*, the *Wall Street Journal*, *The Guardian*, and *The New York* Times portrayed Haniyeh as a "moderate pragmatist," a "peacemaker," and a "leading advocate for a ceasefire."[116] This wasn't just a failure of journalism, it was fiction; it fueled riots in American streets. Haniyeh, a globally recognized terrorist, openly celebrated the October 7th massacre, while candy was being handed out in Palestinian territories in Judea and Samaria. Such reporting not only distorts reality but insults the victims of his violence.

Western journalists are not just ignorant; they actively avoid calling Hamas what it is: a terrorist organization. This hesitancy is reinforced by leaders like Kamala Harris, who publicly opposed the term "Radical Islamic Terrorism" while pandering to a mosque. Words matter, truth matters, and when we avoid sharing facts, it prolongs suffering and war. Hamas is a designated terrorist group by the United States, the United Kingdom, and the European Union. These are facts. Yet media outlets like *The New York Times*, BBC, and Reuters sanitize Hamas as a mere "Palestinian militant group," while Qatari propaganda networks like Al Jazeera glorify them as a "resistance movement." This deliberate manipulation of language is dangerous. Euphemisms do not erase the broken pelvises, the raped women, or the slaughtered families of October 7th. Facts.

Former NPR and CNN political journalist Josh Levs called out news agencies for exhibiting anti-Israel bias in their coverage.

In an opinion piece for *Newsweek*, Levs wrote,

> . . . news organizations still describe Gaza and the West Bank as "the occupied territories." In that phrase, the word "the" is doing the heavy lifting. It indicates that there is one, and only one, "occupation" on Earth to be concerned about. It's a powerful sign of how certain large news organizations have ignored realities worldwide while putting a harsh spotlight only on the tiny dot of a Jewish state.[117]

Levs condemns the media for reporting death-toll numbers provided by The Gaza Health Ministry, which is Hamas, and is spreading misinformation.

Not only is the media mischaracterizing Hamas, news organizations often cite the terrorist organization as a reliable source.

Frustrated and dismayed by the sea of disinformation, I was relieved to find the work of former Associated Press correspondent Matti Friedman. Like Levs, Friedman has publicly called out the biases of mainstream media regarding Israel for decades.

In a 2014 *Tablet* article, "An Insider's Guide to the Most Important Story on Earth," Friedman wrote that the AP once had more than forty staffers assigned to cover Israel and the Palestinian territories (far more than the agency had in China, Russia, or India, or across all fifty countries in sub-Saharan Africa combined). Friedman argued that his colleagues' obsession with the region frequently perpetuated bias against Israel. He claimed journalists no longer prioritize objective truths, and instead push people toward a predetermined "acceptable political outcome."[118]

Bot Farms and Bandwagons

A danger of digital disinformation is how it is engineered to feel overwhelming. A 2021 study from the Oxford Internet Institute found that nearly 47 percent of accounts engaging in political discourse on hot-button issues, like the Israel-Palestine conflict, weren't even real. These bot farms don't just spread propaganda; they manufacture the illusion that fringe narratives are mainstream.[119]

I've seen this firsthand. When I was targeted, it wasn't just by a few bad actors, it was a system working to manipulate perception. Bot-driven harassment campaigns create what's called the "illusion of consensus," a psychological trick known as the "bandwagon effect." The more you see a claim repeated, the more likely you are to believe it's true. Even when it's a lie amplified by fake accounts. This is exactly why we need to be conscious consumers of online information. This is a gentle reminder: we are often engaging in a rigged system designed to exhaust.[120]

Why We're Stuck in the Misinformation Matrix

Multiple phenomena act as enablers that allow misinformation to take root:

Cognitive Ease. Misinformation is often simpler and more emotionally compelling than reality. Our brains prefer easy-to-digest narratives, like the classic hero-versus-villain plot, over more complex, nuanced truths. This makes it easier for a false story to stick.[121]

Tribalism. Misinformation that aligns with a person's ideological or social identity becomes even harder to shake. Admitting you're wrong can feel like betraying your tribe—just look at how people cling to their beliefs about major movements, even when facts challenge them.[122]

Repetition Effect. The more a false claim is repeated, the more familiar it feels—and familiarity breeds belief. This psychological phenomenon, known as the "illusory truth effect," explains why even the most outlandish falsehoods can take root in the public consciousness.

If you hear something enough times, even if it's a blatant lie, your brain begins to accept it as reality.

All of this isn't just an accident of human cognition; it's a tool deliberately wielded by propagandists, extremists, and political operatives. Those who seek to manipulate public perception—whether BDS terrorist sympathizers flooding social media with disinformation or regimes rewriting history—understand that repetition is power. Even Adolf Hitler acknowledged this in *Mein Kampf*, writing that "slogans should be persistently repeated until the very last individual has come to grasp the idea." In the digital age, this strategy has only become more potent. Lies are repeated, retweeted, and algorithmically amplified until they no longer need to be proven. They just need to be heard.[123]

BAD MEDICINE

A dose of Mrs. MD's bad medicine led me to call the FBI, and to dig deeper than I had before, to get to the root of disinformation. To unveil the truth. It reminded me of the way the ground shifts just before something buried is unearthed. The quiet chaos beneath the surface, the tension of something waiting to be revealed.

That image brought me back to Ground Zero: Jerusalem.

There are moments when the world reveals itself in contradictions. When belonging and otherness coexist, when beauty and danger walk hand in hand. When the truth, however buried, begins to rise.

We wove through the narrow streets, moving between conservative Arab quarters and sacred religious Christian and Jewish sites, each space carrying its own weight. The Levant heat pressed thick against my skin, heavy enough to hold me, sharp enough to remind me of everything at stake. My body was mostly covered: a long white dress, my shoulders draped, my mind wide open.

The call to prayer broke the noon silence; it soothed me. I am a xenophile at heart, if anything, drawn to absorb it all—the sounds, the scent of spice in the air, the market's hum, the women with dark kohl eyeliner and even darker burkas. Then we crossed an unmarked street in the Arab neighborhood, cars whipping past, the movement jarring. Our security detail tightening around us.

I walked through a gate and into an excavation site hiding in plain sight, nestled underneath a city of dichotomies. Each step down felt like a quiet defiance against the forces that seek to divide our fractured world. The descent was physical, but it was also something deeper—an unraveling, a peeling back of layers that had long been concealed.

At the base, the air changed. Shade welcomed me, the weight of the city above replaced by a coolness that let my skin breathe. I couldn't help but notice the perfectly weathered stone beneath my feet—smooth, worn by time, its scale both impressive and humbling. As I looked up, Pilgrimage Road stretched before me. A path walked by Jesus more than 2,000 years ago, now unearthed after centuries of burial, right here beneath my sneakers. It had always been here, just under the surface, hidden in plain sight, much like truth itself.

The first stones of this ancient road were rediscovered in 2004, not by design, but by accident: a sewage pipe burst in the east Jerusalem neighborhood of Silwan, revealing history just waiting to be remembered. What was uncovered was more than just a road. It was a lifeline.

A sacred artery leading to the heart of Jerusalem, once pulsing with the footsteps of Jewish pilgrims ascending to the Temple. This was no ordinary path. It was a place of purpose, where merchants called out their wares, priests walked in procession, and travelers from across the ancient world prepared for something greater than themselves.

At its base lay the Pool of Siloam, where weary feet and longing hearts paused for a ritual bath before the final steps to the Temple. Built nearly 2,700 years ago during the reign of King Hezekiah, the pool was a place of purification—both physical and spiritual. It was here, according to Christian tradition, that Jesus restored sight to a blind man, turning the ordinary into the miraculous.

I ran my fingers along the worn stones, feeling their softened edges, their quiet endurance. How many had walked this very path, their prayers rising with the dust beneath their feet? Traders, exiles, worshippers, dreamers—people who had carried their hopes, their burdens, their unshaken belief in something greater. I felt connected to their energy.

Jerusalem is a city that lives in layers. History is not just remembered here—it is rewritten, reclaimed, fought over. It is sacred and contested, a city of both peace and war. To stand on Pilgrimage Road is to feel that tension, to sense the quiet battle between what is seen and what is buried, between what is true and what is told.

And yet, no matter how many times history is rewritten, the stones remain. And they remember.

COUNTERING DISINFORMATION: WHAT WORKS?

Fighting disinformation isn't just about knowing the truth. It requires rewiring how we respond to information in a world designed to manipulate our perceptions. The most effective way to combat falsehoods is to disrupt their influence before they take root. Psychologists and digital literacy experts emphasize the power of *prebunking*: exposing people to the tactics of disinformation before they even encounter it. When you know how deception works, you're far less likely to fall for it.[124]

But awareness alone isn't enough. We need to slow down with cognitive patience—this is taking a breath and thinking critically before reacting—which can significantly curb the spread of false claims. And then there's source transparency. Disinformation thrives on blind trust. Taking a moment to verify where something comes from and questioning its intent can break the cycle before it starts.

But let's be real. This isn't easy. Social media is designed for instant reactions, and outrage spreads faster than facts.

P.A.C.E.

A REFLECTIVE + INTERACTIVE DISCUSSION GUIDE FOR BOOK CLUBS

A Framework for Digital Clarity

P PAUSE

For a discussion starter, think about the last piece of content you shared online, whether a headline, a post, a tweet, or even a meme.

- What made you want to share it?
- What did you want to convey with the post?
- What made it so powerful?
- Did you pause to check the source or verify the claims?
- After posting, did it trigger any strong emotions in people who responded—anger, validation, fear, or outrage?
- How does emotional content spread online, and why do you think that is?

A ANALYZE

Break into small groups. Assign one group to evaluate online content from right-leaning sources, another from heterodox outlets, and the third from left-leaning sources. Choose at least one of these content types:

- A viral headline
- A tweet from a political influencer
- A popular meme
- A breaking news story shared on Instagram or TikTok

Each group should do the following:

- Investigate the original source. Who created it? What are their credentials, expertise, education? What do you think their incentive is for sharing?

- Identify the tone (sensational, neutral, inflammatory, ragey, and so on).

Discussion Points:

- What's the possible agenda behind this content?
- What kind of emotions does it target?
- Is it encouraging critical thinking, or just tribalism and rage-bait?
- How often do we check sources in our daily online habits?
- What would change if we all made analysis part of our digital routine?

C CONTEMPLATE

Personal Journaling Prompts

- Think about your own online habits. What kind of content do you consume the most?
- Do you tend to follow accounts that align with your worldview?
- When was the last time you changed your mind because of something you read online?
- How often do you pause to ask: "Who benefits if I believe this?"
- How can we cultivate intellectual curiosity instead of falling into ideological echo chambers?
- What role does social pressure play? Do we share content to be seen as "good," "aware," "moral" or "on the right side" rather than because it's accurate?

E ENGAGE

Brainstorm practical ways to apply the P.A.C.E. framework in your own lives—online and offline.

Some ideas:

Create a book club fact-checking challenge, where everyone commits to investigating a viral claim before sharing it.

Start a trusted sources list of reliable news outlets, books, and responsible journalists you can all refer to—and actively update.

Practice asking better questions when someone shares inflammatory content:

- Where did this come from?
- Have you seen other credible outlets report this?
- Who benefits if we believe this?

CHAPTER 7

HOW TO PREVENT BLONDE BREAKAGE: CRISIS AND CREATIVITY

Have you ever asked yourself what shapes your will to live, outside of love? Love for your maker, love for your lion or lioness, love for yourself, love for your community and family, even when the world makes it difficult?

For me, it's creativity, certainty, chaos, and rest. A strange combination, I know, but survival rarely looks the way we expect.

The opposite of crisis is often seen as peace. Tranquility, fresh sheets air-dried in the wind, long exhales with no place to rush to, the crash of ocean waves on smooth rocks outside your bedroom window as you drift to sleep, the sound of children's laughter echoing through glimmers of light. The passive and effortless release of a life unburdened.

But reality is rarely so pristine.

The internet, for example, has become a modern-day tent revival. A frenzy of belief, performance, politics, and persuasion. Charlatans sling snake oil under the guise of self-empowerment, repackaging common sense as wisdom and monetizing every life decision we make. The World Wide Web, for all its promises of connection, is also an unbridled feeding ground for predators in the wellness, lifestyle, business, and spiritual spaces—many hiding behind the title of "coach." (I digress, but really, sign up for my class! I kid, ha.)

But crisis has its own pulpit, and it does not take kindly to hesitation. It demands conversion. Not in whispers, but in ultimatums. Adapt or collapse. Reinvent or disappear. Sink or swim. Build or break. Live or die. The choice isn't presented gently; it is baptism by fire, where the only way forward is through. And while reinvention is often painted as a glamorous act of self-determination, a phoenix rising from the ashes, it is, in reality, a last resort. Reinvention is what we do when the ground beneath us crumbles, when the pain of the present moment outweighs the fear of the unknown, when survival demands new architecture. It's when the self we were once before can no longer carry us through what's to come. Reinvention isn't just a choice; it's an act of pure necessity.

It is creativity born from brokenness. When we are fractured, we create the space to be open—to life, light, pain, and purpose, all converging to reconnect us to our wholeness.

Listening to the brokenness is what makes us whole and connected beings in this world.

I always say that *creativity* is simply a fancy word for *listening*.

And according to Rabbi Jonathan Sacks, "to listen is to lead."[125]

In Judaism, the Hebrew word for *listen* is *shema*. Rarely does a word slide perfectly from one language to another, and shema is no exception. It resists a tidy definition, because it holds so much within it. Shema means to hear, but not passively. To listen with your whole being. To show up fully, body and soul, and make space for the voice in front of you. To pay attention, not just to the words spoken, but to the silences between them. To heed what matters. To obey what is just. To understand what is beneath the surface, what is unsaid, what is trembling on the edge of fear.[126]

Shema is the first word I whisper into the soft hush of Friday night, a ritual that signals the shift from the week's momentum into something softer—a doorway into sacred rest. It's a pledge to G-d, but also a pledge to myself. A promise to stop, to breathe, to turn my ear toward what the noise of the week has drowned out. It's an allegiance to tradition, yes, but also to the parts of me that only speak when I am still enough to listen.

We often think of rest as absence. The absence of work, the absence of movement, the absence of urgency. But in Judaism, rest is not empty. It is a presence. A full-bodied listening. A space where creativity, healing, and vision gather, waiting to be heard. Rest is not a passive retreat; it is an active return. A return to self, to spirit, to the still, small voice that hums with our heart beneath the noise of life. The voice that creates, the voice that dreams, the voice that calls you back into alignment.

To listen—truly listen—is the most important gift we can offer someone else. In a world addicted to its own voice, real listening is radical. It is also, perhaps, the most important gift we can offer ourselves. To sit in the quiet and hear our own breath, to notice what rises from within—the uncomfortable truths, the longings, the questions we've been too afraid to ask. Creativity is born from this kind of listening. It does not come from force. It comes from attunement, from resting enough to receive.

Creativity and rest are not opposing forces, but two sides of the same sacred coin. To rest is to listen. To listen is to create. And both are acts of profound faith, faith that the voice within you is worth hearing, that it is leading you somewhere true, that it belongs in this world.

Cancer taught me how to listen. When my body, my life, my very existence felt uncertain, I was forced to slow down, to sit still inside myself, to become quiet enough to hear what I had spent years drowning out. The grief, the fear, the voice that asked, *What if this is it?* But also, beneath all that noise, a whisper of something I hadn't expected: creativity as my form of prayer.

Cancer wasn't just a crisis that took things from me. It gave me something, too. A different kind of attention, a different kind of listening. It taught me how to listen to my life. And in that listening, I discovered my creativity. Not as something external to chase, but as something within me, waiting to be harvested. Something that had always been there, asking for my presence, my permission, my trust.

This is what once landed me on the front cover of *The Tennessean*, our local newspaper—my journey from cancer to creativity. I remember tracing the pages with my fingers, the ink smudging beneath my touch. Marks of a story, stains of survival, and the imprint of transformation. Each page seemed to absorb my experience, as though the paper itself understood what it meant to live on the edge of mortality.

Cancer was my crisis, the catalyst that ignited my new life, the alchemy of survival transforming into expression, courage drawn from the marrow of fear. Even now, I can remember the intrusive thoughts: What if it spreads to my lungs? What does dying feel like? Will I sense it if it comes back? Will I ever bring life into this world? Questions like those give life a sharper edge. They strip you down until all that's left is what's real and honest.

I started my Instagram page during that time, when the cells in my own body were spiraling out of control and the four walls of my home felt like a cage. I needed a place to belong. A space where I could be my own hero, where courage could exist in real time, not polished and perfected, but raw and unfolding. A space where I could gather beauty and light even when the shadows stretched long. Creativity during my crisis became both a refuge and a rebellion, a quiet, deliberate act of reclaiming my voice. A voice that, at the time, was celebrated.

Here's the paradox: one day you're a hero, the next you're a heathen. I live at that intersection, where perception hinges not on objective truths, but on who's telling the story. The social media mean girls prefer "heathen," loudly proclaiming that I'm somehow a threat to democracy. Until, of course, a week later when the Anti-Defamation League in New York City honors me with the 2025 Hero Against Hate award. A recognition rooted in truth, courage, and the refusal to disappear.

Yet here, back in Nashville? *The Tennessean* wouldn't dare put my name on the front cover. Not because my story changed, but because I no longer fit the script they prefer. Because I refuse to perform the palatable, softened version of myself that they're comfortable with. I won't sand down my edges or dilute my convictions to ease the discomfort of a town addicted to the polite pearls of conformity. My defiance, my insistence on owning my own story, has made me an outsider. A voice that won't fold neatly into their narratives. And that is the cost of standing firm in a culture that values curated image over inconvenient truth, spectacle over substance, and silence over complexity.

But I know this: silence has never built anything. Silence has never mended what was broken. Silence has never won a war. Silence has never resolved a crisis.

War tears apart. It fractures landscapes, splits histories, and forces people into allegiances they might never have chosen. Sometimes even against their own families, their own values. But within the heart of a crisis lies an undeniable truth: those who survive must choose what to do with the ruins left behind. Some succumb to despair and continue to live in the past. Others build the plane while they are flying it.

Creativity is rebellion in the face of a crisis. Where there is destruction, it breathes life; where there is fear, it sparks innovation. This is not just a personal insight, it is a collective one, seen through the lens of history and the trials of the Jewish people. It is a truth seen in the heart of Israel itself, a country born out of crisis, surrounded by adversity, yet thriving because of its challenges, not in spite of them.

From its very inception in 1948, Israel was a nation formed in the shadow of destruction. The survivors of the Holocaust, the exiled Jews from neighboring Arab nations, and the immigrant waves who had nowhere else to turn returned to their ancestral homeland where scarcity once ruled. And yet, it is precisely these crises—war, displacement, poverty, and isolation—that sparked a creativity within the Israeli people that transformed the Jewish nation into an epicenter of innovation.

Take, for instance, Israel's agricultural revolution. At the turn of the twentieth century, what is now the State of Israel was little more than barren desert, struggling under Ottoman rule. When Israel declared statehood in 1948, it inherited an environment that was hostile to agriculture. Only 2 percent of the country was forested, and the soil lacked the nutrients needed to support crops.[127] Yet, within decades, Israel's technological ingenuity began to reshape its environment. It became the birthplace of drip irrigation, a revolutionary technology that conserved water while dramatically boosting crop yields.[128] The technology, invented by Simcha Blass, was an act of creative defiance against nature's harshness, and it would go on to change the global agricultural landscape. Today, Israel is a world leader in agricultural technology, exporting its innovations to countries battling droughts and water scarcity around the globe.[129]

This creativity is also seen in Israel's most famous technological marvel: the Iron Dome. Born from the country's need to defend its citizens against constant missile threats, the Iron Dome represents the perfect marriage of military necessity and technological innovation. What began as a response to crisis—building a defense system that could shield civilians from incoming rockets—has evolved into one of the most effective missile defense systems in the world. This triumph not only saved countless lives in Israel but has since been adopted by other nations, including the United States.

Then there's the story of Israel's reforestation efforts, one that often goes overlooked but is no less impressive. At the dawn of the twentieth century, the land that would become Israel was decimated by centuries of neglect under Ottoman and British rule. Israel stands today as the only country to end the twentieth century with more trees than it started with. Over 250 million trees have been planted since 1948, transforming a barren landscape into lush, thriving forests. In 1900, just 2 percent of the land was forested; by the end of the century, this number had grown to 8.5 percent, with trees serving as vital carbon sinks, improving air quality, and providing habitats for wildlife.[130] This is no mere symbol, but a living, breathing testament to the resilience and creativity of a people who refused to be defined by destruction.

In these moments of crisis, Israel has not only rebuilt but reinvented itself. It has created something greater than merely surviving. It has forged an entire ecosystem of innovation and hope. In many ways, Israel's forests are a metaphor for its people. Where others saw desolation, they planted seeds. Where others saw impossibility, they cultivated life. From barren to beautiful, from ashes to innovation. This is what resilience looks like: not just surviving war, but outgrowing it.[131]

During the UN Global Summit Week, I had the opportunity to participate in high-level meetings with the American Jewish Committee, where discussions ranged from strengthening Israeli-Arab relations to the complex warfare unfolding in international courts. I also had the privilege of supporting hostage family members, individuals whose pain was palpable, yet whose resilience in advocating for their loved ones was nothing short of extraordinary. Amid these weighty conversations, my last meeting in New York led to an unexpected and inspiring reunion with a familiar face: Gidi Grinstein and his team from Tikkun Olam Makers (TOM).[132]

TOM is a global Israeli organization dedicated to developing affordable, open-source solutions for often overlooked challenges faced by people with disabilities, the elderly, and underserved communities. When I learned that they were hosting one of their annual TOM Makeathon events at Vanderbilt University, I knew I had to be part of it. I offered my photography skills to capture the behind-the-scenes moments of innovation in action.

The event was a testament to the power of creativity, collaboration, and purpose-driven problem-solving. Students, engineers, and designers came together to address real needs within the Nashville community, transforming ideas into tangible solutions. Among the prototypes developed were an ergonomic button-activated camera, physical therapy devices, a voice-activated door opener and lock, adaptable strollers, customized wheelchairs, a lightweight desk for a child with muscular dystrophy, and a brace for hypermobility. What struck me most was not just the ingenuity of the solutions but the spirit behind them—an unwavering commitment to making life easier for others, to seeing a problem and saying: we can fix this. Each design was documented and added to TOM's open-source marketplace, ensuring that people across the world could replicate and improve on them, free of charge.

That weekend was a powerful reminder that healing doesn't just happen in grand gestures or diplomatic agreements. It happens in the small, everyday acts of repair. Creativity is not just an artistic expression; it is a survival instinct, a force for change that turns crisis into progress. Watching these innovators work reaffirmed my belief that creation is the antidote to destruction. When we build something new, whether it's a device that restores independence, a movement that reclaims a voice, or a technology that safeguards lives, we are resisting despair.

To be creative is simply to be human. It transcends political, national, and religious lines for the sake of something greater: humanity itself. This is the same creative energy flowing through the veins of the global Jewish community, a people who have been repeatedly tested by crisis, yet always find a way to build. Whether through the arts, technology, education, or social change, Jewish communities around the world have harnessed their creativity as a powerful tool for resistance against antisemitism. In the face of prejudice and hatred, Jewish artists, thinkers, and innovators have turned their pain into progress, their suffering into stories that reshape society.

Where there is destruction, there is the potential for creation. The past is written in the ruins of what came before, but the future is built by those who dare to visualize something new. This is what makes the Jewish experience so profoundly resilient: even in the face of war and hardship, we do not remain silent. We create. We build. And we will continue to do so, because silence has never won a war. But creativity, defiance, and renewal? These are the forces that reshape the world.

P.A.C.E.

A REFLECTIVE + INTERACTIVE DISCUSSION GUIDE FOR BOOK CLUBS

A Framework for Transmuting Crisis into Creativity

P PAUSE

The Art of Full-Body Listening

The first step is not to act, but to listen, fully, deeply, and with your entire being. In Judaism, the word "shema" doesn't just mean "hear." It means to listen with every part of your being. It's a full-body experience, a grounding exercise, a radical presence in a world addicted to noise and its own voice.

So try this: Wherever you are right now, pause. Breathe in. Breathe out. Now, use all five senses:

- What do you hear? The hum of a fridge? The wind? The absence of sound?
- What do you taste? Coffee? Mint? The salt of an earlier tear?
- What do you smell?
- What do you see, not just directly in front of you, but in the periphery?
- What do you feel beneath your feet? What is your hand resting on?

Place your right hand over your heart, your left on your stomach. Feel the weight of being here, now.

And this week, when a friend speaks, don't rush to respond. Don't match their story with one of your own. Hold space. Let silence do the work. Listening is an act of love.

A ANALYZE

The Alchemy of Challenge

Crisis does not ask politely for our attention. It arrives like an uninvited guest, upending everything we thought was certain. It gives ultimatums: adapt or collapse, sink or swim, build or break. But within every crisis is an opportunity—a doorway to something else—for courage and growth.

Think of the artists who created during exile. The families who, after unimaginable loss, built new homes, new traditions, and new futures.

Now ask yourself:

1. What challenge in your life is demanding your attention right now?
2. Where are you resisting change?
3. If you can look at the challenge in your life as an invitation, what is it asking you to do, and who is it asking you to become?

Write it down. Say it out loud. Resistance is often a compass. Follow where it leads.

C CONTEMPLATE

Reverse Engineering Your Courage

Creativity is not just an expression; it is an act of courage. It is looking at your life—your fears, your losses, your desires—and asking: Who within my highest self do I need to become to start building a new future?

If you had to paint a picture of your ideal life, what would it look like? Now, work backward.

- What steps would have to be taken to get there?
- What risks would have to be embraced?
- How can you coexist with your fear to keep you moving forward?
- What comforts would have to be sacrificed?

A Jewish proverb says: "A dream that is not interpreted is like a letter that is never opened." What dreams are waiting inside you, sealed, unopened?

E ENGAGE

Creative Courage as Daily Action

In *The New Southern Style*, I discuss my philosophy around creative courage: believing in a vision so much greater than yourself when your current reality doesn't reflect it—yet. This requires clarity and taking action in the direction of your vision each day. It is the ultimate act of self-love and co-creation with your higher power, where you show up and build even in the face of fear, when the vision you have for yourself demands new architecture.

What is one seed you can plant today? One small, daily action that moves you toward your vision?

Maybe it's a sentence written, a conversation started, an email sent, a boundary set, a story told. Maybe it's saying "yes" to an idea that scares you or "no" to something that no longer serves you, or walking away from someone holding you back.

Because change—true, lasting change—is not built in grand, sweeping gestures. It is built in the quiet, daily commitment to something larger than yourself when you are afraid and when you are uncomfortable. It's making new decisions that you've never made before.

So what is your first step? Name it. Take it. The world is waiting.

WHITE.

BLONDE.

JEW.

CHAPTER 8

HE DOESN'T WANT JEWISH CHILDREN

His words came slowly, deliberate yet heavy, unraveling the past ten years of our marriage in fragments that flashed through my mind in an instant: the sexless nights, the quiet mornings after loud arguments, his drinking, the emotional abuse, and the constant fear that the other shoe would drop.

I stood frozen in the kitchen, gripping the edge of the cold marble countertop, bracing myself against the truth I could no longer outrun. And then, all at once, the full weight of his words crashed over me, shattering the last bit of hope I'd held on to: "I don't want Jewish children."

It's human nature to crave connection and closeness when words of pain and finality echo in your ears, like instinctively reaching for a warm sweater just as the chill of fall settles in.

Still jet-lagged from the eight-hour time difference with Israel, my body felt heavy, but my mind was restless, racing through every memory, desperate to pinpoint what I had missed.

How could I have been so blind? How many years of my life had I just thrown away?

Each breath came shallow. I told myself to inhale, but it felt like the air had been drained from my lungs, like I had nothing left to give, and nothing left to lose. Everything around me was unraveling, and all I could do was stand there, paralyzed, as the fragments of my life drifted away like autumn leaves, scattering at my feet.

He wasn't antisemitic. I knew that for certain. But had the suffering he'd witnessed overwhelmed him?

Did the pain he saw me endure make him shy away? Was it fear, not hate, that shaped his words? Fear that our children will be burdened with the weight of a history they didn't choose but cannot escape?

Or had something changed in him, something I had overlooked, buried beneath years of silence and unresolved fractures?

Living in the diaspora, outside of Israel, I've fought to push back against harmful narratives, to educate, and to resist. But to him, any kind of religion felt more like indoctrination. Suffocation. As a scientist and surgeon, he had little patience and often wrestled with matters of faith, which lie at the heart of my ethno-cultural identity.

Being Jewish isn't something I can put on or take off; it's woven into the very fabric of my being. My passion declares it. My creativity honors it. My sense of justice defends it. My ancestors died for it. The empty spaces in my family tree mourn for it. My DNA carries the proof of my people's origins, woven into me like an ancestral thread, providing strength and resilience. Did he truly believe this was something I could simply shed, like a coat tossed aside?

When we were first married, we had conversations about how we'd raise our children. My version of "Jewish Light" felt like an easy compromise at the time: Sunday School, Hebrew School, Bar and Bat Mitzvahs for the kids, and showing up for the High Holidays. I wanted to infuse just enough to honor tradition without it becoming our whole life. It felt reasonable. Manageable. But then, all of a sudden, he didn't want it. Any of it.

And then when the world shifted, so did I.

I knew, without a doubt, what I needed for the future of my Jewish children. I needed them to know who they are—not just in moments of celebration, but in moments of challenge. I needed them to carry the resilience, the joy, and the divinity of their heritage. To understand the weight and wonder of where they come from, and why it matters.

This wasn't just about compromise; it was about something deeper. Something that had been quietly stirring inside me all along. Tradition was no longer just a checklist of rituals; it was a lifeline, a responsibility, a shield. A thread connecting me to generations before and a foundation for the ones to come. It wasn't about convenience anymore; it was about survival. I could feel it in every breaking-news alert, in every uneasy pause, in every glance that lingered a second too long in the wrong places.

I needed them to hold their history with pride, even in a world that too often demands they leave it at the door.

I needed to be with a partner who understood how high the stakes are for our family.

Philosopher, luminary, and scholar Rabbi Jonathan Sacks taught that becoming a parent is the closest we come to experiencing G-d, bringing life into the world through love and co-creation.[133] Though I am childless as I write this, I have birthed creativity and mothered others in deeply meaningful ways. I've surrendered to seasons of uncertainty, holding space with an open heart and open hands, trusting what has yet to unfold. In these moments of release, I've drawn closer to the light of the Creator, embracing faith, pain, and hope. These moments not only connect us to G-d or the Universe, however we understand that presence, but also offer us a lifeline to something larger than ourselves.

The rhythms of life and death open deeper channels to the Divine. It's through this cycle that I find myself mothering through three wars: the relentless war in Israel, the ideological battle sweeping the West, and the quiet, personal war of divorce, waged between two hearts, now separated by the silence of an empty home in the South. These swirling conflicts carried me to the City of Angels, seeking acts of resistance and renewal.

Like my ancestors, I rebel through storytelling, through truth, through my photos and creativity. It is how I throw stones into the ideological world I wish to change. And in this act, I find a strange sense of freedom. Each stone of resistance becomes a step forward, shaping and accumulating, forming a walkable path, one more stable than the road behind me, one that feels aligned with who I am becoming. It's a path where choice, not circumstance, defines the way forward.

Every stone is weighted with desire, responsibility, and an undeniable need for the building blocks of a family of my own, family grounded in stories of the past that sharpen the tools we use to shape the future.

It was this journey that led me to the Holocaust Museum in Los Angeles, where my family's history lives not merely as an echo but as a guiding light. The museum selected me to help promote a new art exhibit titled "To Paint Is to Live," which explores art as a form of resistance in Theresienstadt. My selection for this project stemmed from my own fight against adversity during my battle with cancer, when I was rebelling against the loss of control over my body and finding freedom through the lens of my camera. With each click of the shutter, I created a framework and built a community where I could share my journey and advocate for my community whenever injustice surfaced.

Much like cancer with its unregulated and rapid cell divisions, antisemitism follows a similar, viral trajectory in societies—rapid, volatile, and destructive. It spreads insidiously, infecting minds and communities, feeding on ignorance and fear. Just as unchecked cell growth can lead to devastating consequences, the unchecked spread of antisemitism can erode the very foundations of our social fabric, creating divisions and perpetuating hate.

Two dear friends, the granddaughters of survivors, Amanda Markowitz and Lindsay Schechter, greeted me at the museum as an armed security guard opened the large glass doors. The modern building felt hollow, despite the heavy history it held. Concrete floors and walls echoed our voices, the only proof of life in the space. Every detail in the design was deliberate: the ceiling gradually lowered, and the hallways narrowed, guiding you deeper into the profound pain of World War II.

I began walking through the museum's halls, passing glass cases filled with photos of families, snapshots of everyday Jewish life in Europe before the war's darkness descended. These images captured a fragile normalcy, faces that could have been my own relatives, filled with hopes and routines before being swallowed by history's darkest chapter.

I paused before a wall covered in newspaper clippings, each headline capturing the lies and propaganda that twisted reality for millions.

The accusations and propaganda techniques felt unsettlingly familiar. Precursors of today's distortions, of the modern-day blood libels and accusations of genocide, colonialism, and apartheid infiltrating the media and international courts.

A knot formed in my stomach as I imagined what it must have been like for a young Jewish woman in the 1940s, watching as the world around her warped under the weight of such lies.

As I moved deeper into the exhibit, the halls narrowed, and towering images of children's shoes piled high filled my view, pressing against the shallow ceiling. Photos of bodies layered upon one another stirred flashbacks of a recent trip to Israel, where I listened to Rafaela, a survivor who hid beneath the dead in a bunker, their bodies both concealing and shielding her from bullets for hours.

This is her testimony:

> We ran toward the road shelter. We were the first inside. Eventually, forty of us packed in, trying to breathe, trying to stay silent. Then the gunfire started. We could hear them—see them. The terrorists came in waves, throwing Molotov cocktails, hand grenades, and gas grenades. People around me started dying. The top layers of bodies absorbed the impact.
>
> After each round of grenades, they stormed in, shooting anyone still alive. Then they would leave—waiting just long enough

for the survivors to think it was safe to escape. And when they did, I heard the gunshots. One by one, they were executed.

Just outside the bunker, they built a fire of human bodies. They raped those who tried to flee and burned them alive. A girl near me panicked, but the screams had already quieted. The weight of the dead covered us and kept us alive. And so, we survived.

Her voice trembled but did not break. Her words carried the weight of memory, of terror, of the unbearable price of survival.

These stories, attached to such raw visuals, were familiar. I'd grown up with them, tragic yet woven into my family's legacy. They felt like an old friend, a shadow in the family tree where lives and stories had been cut short. Yet here, they struck me with new importance, the memories pushing me through tight walls that seemed to close in, mirroring the suffocating weight of what Jews around the world are experiencing today.

Finally, I reached the last exhibit, the one I flew in for. I felt strangely numb, a restrained anger simmering underneath my navy blue blazer. It was the kind of anger that was not about emotion but about truth, an awareness that this history still reverberates and demands to be punched in the throat.

As I turned the corner to the "To Paint Is to Live" Theresienstadt exhibit, the walls layered with sketches, architectural drawings of the camp, paintings on potato sacks met me with ease.[134]

I exhaled.

Theresienstadt, or Terezín, stands as one of history's most chilling examples of deception and resilience.

Established by the Nazis in Czechoslovakia, this ghetto-camp was presented as a "model ghetto." Jewish prisoners were supposedly allowed to live freely. In reality, the camp was a place that bred tremendous suffering and forced labor, and it was a transit point to extermination camps.

In 1944 the International Red Cross went to Theresienstadt to inspect the conditions, after hearing murmurings of the Germans' murdering of Jews.

The Nazis orchestrated an elaborate charade for the Red Cross, going so far as to plant flowers, build storefronts, and produce a propaganda film depicting a *Truman Show*-esque idyllic Jewish spa-like town where elderly Jews could retire.

Starving, malnourished, and broken bodies were deliberately hidden from view, and shockingly, the Red Cross bought into the Nazi charade. At Theresienstadt, the façade worked. The visiting delegates failed to see beyond the carefully curated illusion of normalcy and left without questioning the camp's true purpose as a transit hub for mass extermination.

History, however, reveals a far worse reality: by the war's end, 33,000 Jews had perished within the camp's walls. Years later, concealed documents surfaced, exposing that the Red Cross had access to evidence of the atrocities yet chose not to act.[135] They knew genocide was unfolding—a devastating failure that echoes in the suffering we see today. Not once since October 7th has the Red Cross provided humanitarian aid, medical care, or even checked on the hostages. Silence then. Silence now.[136]

Beneath the thin veneer of Nazi propaganda, Theresienstadt became an unexpected epicenter of artistic resistance. A testament to the indomitable spirit of its prisoners.

Yet even amid the devastation, an extraordinary act of defiance unfolded. Imprisoned Jewish luminaries documented their harrowing experiences and clung to their humanity and history through art that would outlive the horrors of their death.

In secret, they created music, art, and writings that bore witness to the brutal reality of life under Nazi rule, defying efforts to strip away their humanity and identity. Their creations left behind a testament of their resilience, exposing the Nazi lie and, eventually, the world's willingness to look away.

Then on February 27th, 2024, eighty years after the camp's inception, I stood in front of those very pieces. As I looked at the work I felt a familiar sense of home, as if my ancestors were standing beside me, holding my hand, their presence quiet, and enduring.

Amanda was interviewing me, her questions centering on creativity, but my focus kept slipping away. My mind wandered, drawn into the haunting and beautiful artwork that lined the walls. It was as if, somehow, my family's presence lingered here, their stories silently preserved in the lines, shadows, and shades of each piece. The art seemed to breathe with a life that I recognized, whispering memories that felt all too close.

The work of Czech architect Fred Beckmann (1908–1989) filled the room. His meticulously drawn sketches of the buildings in Theresienstadt were created under the most dire conditions. Each drawing was not only a piece of art but an act of defiance, capturing the truth and grim reality of the camps with every pen stroke.

As I gazed at his scenes, I couldn't help but wonder: Were my relatives nearby as Beckmann sketched in secret? Were they among the faceless figures etched into the yellowed paper, shadows caught in a moment of history?

How thin had they become? Were their bodies gaunt with hunger? What fragments of hope did they clutch to, even as everything was stripped away?

The drawings spoke more than their words ever could; they were lines etched in defiance of erasure, a testament that they had existed, that they mattered, that I matter.

A sudden warm tear rolled down my cheek and pulled me back into the present with Amanda and Lindsay. I paused, letting the weight of the moment settle before sharing where my mind had drifted, to a space filled with echoes of sacrifice, whispers carrying a truth I couldn't ignore: I stand here because of their bravery. Now it is our turn to carry courage forward, to honor their spirits.

Their creativity and defiance, their insistence on being seen and remembered, has become my torch to bear. In that space, art was more than memory; it was a weapon against forgetting, a lifeline connecting the past to the present. This exhibit was not a collection of relics; it was a sacred repository of lives that could have been my own, reminding me that the fight to preserve truth is far from over.

The art of Theresienstadt is a legacy of courage under terror and a reminder that, even in the darkest of times, the human spirit finds ways to resist, to remember, and to reveal the truth.

Before we left the grounds, Lindsay asked if I wanted to visit the children's memorial. The armed guard reopened the door for us, and we stepped outside into the fading light. The sun was setting, casting a warm glow that felt almost at odds with the heavy air.

I took a deep breath, letting the coolness fill my lungs, craving the life force that pulsed around us. I exhaled slowly, trying to steady myself. As we walked, Lindsay softly began recounting the heartbreaking numbers: 1.5 million children lost in the Holocaust.[137]

The memorial itself was smaller than the main museum, a quiet, enclosed space where curved concrete walls wrapped around us like an embrace. These walls were punctured with millions of tiny holes, each varying in size, 1.2 million in total, symbolizing the children whose lives were cut short.[138]

Much like the Kotel in Jerusalem, visitors could slip notes or prayers into the openings, each one a whispered plea or a silent remembrance. In the center of the wall, someone had carefully arranged their rolled-up notes into the shape of a heart.

I left Lindsay and Amanda behind, drawn toward that heart. As I approached, it felt as though the weight of history pressed in from all sides, thick in the air around me. I sat quietly, taking in the stillness, the way the light moved delicately across the space. The emptiness felt profound, a silence of overwhelming grief that mirrored the lives of the children taken on October 7th. Yet, within that sorrow, there was also a sense of something enduring, something hopeful, a torch that, against all odds, has not been extinguished.

For me, that torch is carried through my books, my photography, and my creative work, attempts to document and honor the past while breathing life into the present. But I know that the truest and most lasting flame will be carried by my future Jewish child, who will take forward what I have begun and what our ancestors so fiercely preserved.

Our children are not just our future; they are the continuation of a story that must never be allowed to end.

While art, creativity, and the love we pour into our partners and those we nurture in this world may not shield us from the battles around us or the wars we wage within, they offer something truly profound: a way to shape light that pierces even the darkest days. These expressions, our words, our art, our legacies—are how we leave our mark on the world long after we're gone. They are threads that weave through generations, echoes of who we are, and reminders of the values we hold dear.

ANOTHER POGROM

I was sitting in the tub after a long day. The room was dark except for the soft flicker of candles. The bubbles were piled high around me, and for a moment, I allowed myself to sink into the stillness, to release the tension in my body. My eyes closed, and just as I felt myself letting go, I heard the familiar ding of my phone. *Ugh, I really need to start turning off notifications.*

I reached for the phone anyway, hoping it was nothing urgent. The message was from my best friend: "The scenes out of Amsterdam. So horrible. So sad."

A chill ran through me. My heart quickened, and I felt the bubble of peace I was trying to cultivate pop. I immediately went to X because, as I've learned, the mainstream news is too slow, too selective, too skewed, too silent. My feed was filled with videos, raw, unfiltered, and devastating.

I couldn't believe what I was watching unfold in real time: an actual pogrom happening in 2024.[139]

The word "pogrom" is Russian for "to wreak havoc," and refers to violent attacks on Jewish communities, which occurred during anti-Jewish riots in Odessa in 1821.[140]

During the Holocaust, under Adolf Hitler's rule, a violent pogrom started on November 9th, 1938, and became known as Kristallnacht, or the "Night of Broken Glass," due to the widespread destruction of Jewish homes and synagogues, marked by shattered glass on the streets and sidewalks.[141]

More than eighty years later nearly to the date, on November 8th, 2024, a live-streamed Jewish pogrom in Amsterdam happened, where antisemitic violence erupted during a soccer match between the Israeli team Maccabi Tel Aviv and the Dutch team Ajax Amsterdam. Riots broke out, including assaults on Jewish bodies. As Israel National News reported:

> "They waited in groups at every corner, and as soon as they recognized Jews, they started chasing them. Others waited near hotels and near the casino and larger groups, and there they also attacked fans and others drove by with cars and did not stop honking near hotels in which Israelis were staying."[142]

This was not random. Whispers of collusion pointed to corrupt police officers and hotel staff aiding the manhunt for Jews. Stabbings, human bodies thrown from bridges into icy waters, and calculated attacks unfolded in what was, in the most chilling sense, a coordinated Jew hunt. The AJC reported:

> Dutch authorities revealed that the attack was far from spontaneous; it had been meticulously orchestrated via WhatsApp, with a group chat calling for a "Jew hunt." Targeting Jews everywhere is exactly what former Hamas head Ismail Haniyeh meant when he called to "globalize the intifada."[143]

I responded to my best friend, "I'm in tears." Their reply was instant: "I am so sorry." I typed back, "I just wrote about the Holocaust today. It is too much." I watched the three dots appear, and then: "So maddening." My fingers hovered over the screen, raging. "From the propaganda to calculated incidents like this—this is how it begins," I wrote.

This is Europe right now, I thought. It was happening. Planes from Israel were being chartered to Amsterdam to rescue Jews. Once again,

Israel was stepping in to protect my brothers' and sisters' lives on European soil.

BEING JEWISH THIS DECADE

Imagine it: you go to a soccer game with friends, your family. The laughter, the cheers, the joy wells up around you. And then, as you leave, you're suddenly hunted by a pro-Jihadi mob armed with knives, cars used as weapons, your body flung into the cold waters of the canal, beaten and broken.

This is what it's like being Jewish now.

And the horror doesn't stop there. Taxi drivers refuse to take Jews to safety. Hotel staff betray their guests, disclosing where Jews are staying. Police either stand by silently or, worse, actively join in the violence. Those who should offer protection become part of the nightmare, turning what should be a place of refuge into a trap. In that moment, safety in Europe is stripped away, revealing a darkness that's all too familiar, and all too real.

I turned to my community, the one I have built brick by brick over the years, across social media feeds and book pages, and tried to share what I was seeing in a way that they might understand. I wanted them to see themselves in this story because, G-d forbid, this could be any of us.

And yet, the list of names ran through my mind—the Glennon Doyles, the Amanda Sealeses, the Ericka Harts, and the Candace Owenses of the world—voices with massive followings who have irresponsibly stoked the flames, making false claims of genocide and peddling narratives that conflate complex geopolitical issues with race.

This is not just ignorance; it's a willful distortion that legitimizes hate and gives permission to those who seek to harm Jews. It's the acceptance of antisemitism in a society that turns a blind eye to violence against Jews. These people with platforms, who have never faced the reality of what they're encouraging, have blood on their hands.

The Amsterdam pogrom was not just an isolated incident; it was calculated and coordinated. It was the darkness rising again in the same places where our ancestors were once hunted. And yet, the world remained eerily silent.

I wondered how many more dings of my phone it would take for the world to wake up. How many more videos must we witness before we understand that history is not staying in the past? Because here we were, a month after honoring the massacre of Jewish bodies on October 7th, watching another chapter unfold, this time in the heart of Europe.

P.A.C.E.

A REFLECTIVE + INTERACTIVE DISCUSSION GUIDE FOR BOOK CLUBS

He Doesn't Want Jewish Children

P PAUSE

Women, War, and the Weight of Marriage

This chapter began by exploring the roles of women—mothers, wives, daughters—living under the weight of survival, war, expectation, and inherited responsibility. The moment of reckoning is when tradition is no longer just a checklist of rituals, but a lifeline, a shield. It's no longer about compromise or convenience, but survival. We see how deeply personal relationships are interwoven with global and historical events. Before diving in, let's pause.

1. What inherited expectations—from family, culture, or history—shape how you understand your role in relationships?
2. Share a phrase or story passed down from the women in your family about survival. How do these stories resonate with your own experiences?
3. Are these stories about resilience, silence, endurance, or sacrifice?
4. What steps can you take to feel divinely protected or guided from your ancestors? This is for you to pull resilience from—gifts that are known to you.

Group Activity

As a group, reflect on how history, generational trauma, and societal expectations shape how we show up in relationships today. Take turns sharing how your family history influences the way you love, fight, or stay silent. What tools have you inherited for survival, whether they are emotional, mental, or physical? Discuss how these tools either support or challenge your current relationships.

A ANALYZE

When World Events Sit at the Kitchen Table

This chapter doesn't just focus on a personal story. It threads in the contemporary and historical propaganda in Theresienstadt, creativity, war, and generational trauma. It teaches us that personal lives are rarely isolated from global events.

Discussion Questions

1. What does it mean to stand firm in the middle of a personal storm while facing global upheaval, especially knowing your ancestors endured unimaginable suffering?
2. Does the historical weight give you strength, or does it feel like a burden?

Group Exercises

- In small groups, discuss how global historical events continue to shape and influence your personal relationships today.
- Reflect on how inherited trauma intersects with your desire to move forward. Do you ever feel as though history pulls you backward, influencing your ability to engage in the present?
- Consider whether your capacity to confront adversity is shaped by your gender, family history, or cultural background.

C CONTEMPLATE

In this chapter, I surrender. My silence becomes both an act of survival and a way to regroup. When has your body frozen in a similar way? Have you ever used silence as a tool to reclaim your power before finding your voice again?

Journal Exercise: Stillness, Surrender, and Finding Your Voice

- What does surrendering mean to you as a form of power?
- When have you stayed still in overwhelming moments? Did it feel like survival or power? How did finding your voice shift that experience?
- How does inherited trauma train our bodies to go inward? How has silence protected you in the past? What would it feel like to unlearn that and speak out instead?
- Is silence always a weakness, or can it be a weapon? How can you reclaim silence as a tool of empowerment? When does silence become an act of resistance rather than suppression?

Writing Prompt (Solo or Group)

Write a legacy letter to an ancestor, a future daughter, your inner child, or to your future self. Share how you will show up through this time in history and where you will continue to cultivate both surrender and power. Take a moment to reflect on your own legacy. Consider the resilience of those who came before you. Reflect on the strength it took to survive everything you have endured. Let your words be forged in truth, like stones laid to pave a path forward.

Group Activity

Share your legacy letter with the group, if comfortable. Discuss how writing this letter helped you reclaim your voice, and whether silence was something you inherited or learned as a tool for survival.

E ENGAGE

This chapter is a call to action for women to rewrite their own stories and break free from the constraints of history. You have the power to reclaim your voice and your narrative—to shape your life, your relationships, and your role in the world. The weight of the past doesn't have to define your future. We stand at a moment in history where your choices, your voice, and your actions can break generational patterns of pain, trauma, and silence.

Prompts for Action

1. What patterns from the past have shaped who you are today? How can you actively rewrite these patterns moving forward?
2. Think about a time when you stepped into your full power. What did that look like, and how did it shift your life?
3. In what ways can you use your voice today to challenge the repeating cycles of history and claim a different path for the future?

Group or Individual Exercise

Take a moment to share with the group or reflect individually: What does owning your power look like? How will you rewrite your story today? Make a list of concrete actions you will take to rewrite your legacy.

CHAPTER 9

MOBILIZING AMERICA AND ANTISEMITISM

What's more American than off-roading in a Ford pickup truck on a sunbaked back road? Think slow summers, old front porches, and neighbors who wave as they pass. Kids chasing fireflies barefoot in yards, the smell of barbecue drifting through the air while Chris Stapleton hums from the console of an old F-150.

To many, Ford Motor Company stands as a symbol of American innovation and industry. Its founder, Henry Ford, revolutionized manufacturing and put America on wheels, forever changing the nation's economic landscape.

At the end of 2024, just one day before the clock struck midnight to usher in a new year, Ford Motor Company's X account posted three shocking messages: "All Eyes on Gaza," "Israel is a Terrorist State," and "Free Palestine."

These unsettling statements served as a chilling reminder of what the coming year could hold if the persistent tide of antisemitism remained unchecked.

Many see this corporation as the quintessential "All-American" brand, yet these tweets felt less like a shocking departure and more like a homecoming. Very on brand. Not just to its location, but to a narrative deeply woven into its history. Soon after, Ford Motor Company issued a statement claiming its account had been compromised, distancing itself from the posts and denying responsibility.

No apologies (other than for "any confusion it caused"), no accountability, no reaffirmation of American values—just a glaring void where Western democratic principles could have been typed.

Yet, this incident demands deeper scrutiny, not just of Ford's historical legacy of Jew hatred, but of America's enduring conversation with antisemitism and its modern manifestations.

Henry Ford's legacy is stained by his relentless promotion of antisemitic propaganda, a force that fueled the prejudices of his time and lingers today in different forms. In a city, Dearborn, Michigan, where new ideologies of Islamism echo old hatreds of Nazism, the company's compromised account serves as an obvious reminder of how antisemitism adapts and shifts, offering an opportunity to reflect on its enduring presence in our society.

HENRY FORD AND THE DEARBORN INDEPENDENT

In 1919, Henry Ford purchased the *Dearborn Independent*,[144] transforming the newspaper into a megaphone for his antisemitic ideology. For nearly a decade, the paper published a series of inflammatory articles accusing Jews of controlling global finance, media, and politics (I really wish this were the case. A lot of pain would have been spared the past few years, were this true).

Ford seized every opportunity to scapegoat Jews for society's "perceived ills," weaving together baseless accusations and hate.

The Dearborn Independent also reprinted sections of the Protocols of the Elders of Zion—think of this as the antisemitic Bible. These lies were republished in the newspaper and later compiled into Ford's book, *The International Jew: The World's Foremost Problem*. Despite being fiction and baseless, these conspiracy theories gained international momentum, traveling far beyond American borders, cementing Ford as a key figure in the spread of modern antisemitism.

Henry Ford's antisemitic beliefs didn't stop with his personal ideas; they infiltrated his business, leaving a stain on his corporate legacy (or an invitation into jihadism). At Ford Motor Company, reports suggest that both Jewish and Black applicants were intentionally excluded through discriminatory hiring practices. This was a reflection of a broader societal attitude toward Jews in the early twentieth century in the West, a time when barriers to equality for the Jewish community were not just social but institutional.

Henry Ford and Hitler: BFFs

Ford Motor Company has tried to separate itself from this dark history *(ish)*, but it's a reminder of what happens when people stay silent in the face of hate.

Adolf Hitler openly admired Henry Ford's antisemitic ideologies, going so far as to reference Ford as an inspiration in *Mein Kampf*.[145]

Can you imagine? Let that sink in.

Also, can we stop naming our children after Henry Ford?

Hitler was such a fan that he kept a portrait of Ford displayed in his office.

The connection doesn't stop there. In 1938, Nazi Germany awarded Ford the Grand Cross of the German Eagle, their highest honor, and praised his so-called "humanitarian ideals" and "devotion to peace."[146] The chilling irony of this recognition speaks volumes about the alignment of Ford's beliefs with the propaganda fueling one of history's darkest chapters.

Antisemitism in Ford's Business Practices

The shadow of Ford's antisemitism stretched even further during World War II, as his company's European subsidiaries were accused of *actively participating* with the Nazi regime. Allegations include the use of forced labor and supplying vehicles and parts that facilitated death.[147]

AMERICA'S ANTISEMITISM ATTITUDE

Ford's legacy casts a long and unsettling shadow over today's realities. Where the *Dearborn Independent* once spread antisemitic propaganda, the streets of Dearborn, Michigan, now echo with loud calls in Arabic of "Death to Israel" and "Death to America." Social media, the modern megaphone for misinformation, amplifies the same insidious rhetoric, turning old lies into viral conspiracies. From false cries of "Apartheid" to recycled accusations of secret Jewish cabals and calls for the end of Zionism, Ford's Jew-hating tropes haven't disappeared. They've been supercharged by algorithms and weaponized through coordinated BDS propaganda campaigns. And like it or not, we're all unwilling guests at this grotesque spectacle.

We've seen this most recently in the spring of 2024 in the very city that hosts Ford's headquarters, where protestors sang praises for terrorists and called for the destruction of Israel.

The ADL reported:

> At a Quds Day demonstration that attracted hundreds of attendees outside the Henry Ford Centennial Library in Dearborn, MI on April 5, protesters chanted, in Arabic, "Death to Israel" and "Death to America." A protester proudly displayed an image of Iran's Ayatollah Khomeini while others held signs with messages that included "The Zionist entity has no right to exist" and "From the river to the sea! Expel all occupiers."[148]

Activist Tarek Bazzi began the event by asking the crowd to pray for "the victory of the resistance" and referred to "the resistance fighters [who] engage in battle with this godless, satanic cancer that is called Israel." Bazzi also stated that "the chant, 'death to Israel,' has become the most logical chant shouted across the world today."[149]

The shocking posts from Ford's X account, whether the result of a hack or deliberate action, highlight how seamlessly antisemitism infiltrates public discourse. These statements mirror current culture, falsely portraying Israel as a singular villain while erasing the nuanced realities of an eight-front proxy war orchestrated by the Iranian regime. Such rhetoric thrives in an environment where Jew hatred is increasingly normalized, underscoring the critical need to challenge it at every turn.

It feels like I'm trapped in a fishbowl, my voice muted by the water around me. No one can hear me, yet I see everything unfolding with so much clarity. And maybe this is how my ancestors felt in Europe, watching the tides turn, screaming into silence, until it was too late.

Confronting America's "All-American" Myth

Ford Motor Company's history reveals the fragility of the "All-American" identity. Henry Ford's antisemitism was not an anomaly; it was a reflection of mainstream prejudices in his time. Today, America struggles with the same challenge, defining its values and identity in the face of dormant hate.

To be "All-American" could mean embracing pluralism and accepting all people. Yet, as antisemitic incidents rise and public figures perpetuate dangerous rhetoric, America risks repeating the errors of Ford's era. The nation's commitment to combating antisemitism must be as relentless as Ford's commitment was to spreading it.

Representative Rashida Tlaib, the Palestinian-American congresswoman from Michigan, recently called the slogan "From the River to the Sea" an "aspirational call for freedom, human rights, and peaceful coexistence."

As the Foundation for Defense of Democracies (FDD) aptly noted, this slogan has long signaled a violent, genocidal intent, not a peaceful call for coexistence.[150]

A willful distortion of history, the true purpose of the slogan "From the River to the Sea" is to reject any Jewish presence or control over land between the Jordan River and the Mediterranean Sea.

In 1980, Yasser Arafat made it clear when he declared, "The victorious march will continue until the flag of Palestine is raised above Jerusalem and above the whole area of Palestine from the River to the Sea."[151]

On October 7th, Hamas demonstrated what "From the River to the Sea" really means in practice. Their brutal actions left no ambiguity, regardless of how some protesters may choose to interpret it in theory.[152]

MOVING FORWARD

Ford's antisemitic legacy stands as both a cautionary tale and a call to action. It underscores a critical truth: progress is neither linear nor guaranteed. Combating antisemitism requires vigilance, proactive education, and consistent accountability.

For the Jewish community, this moment calls for more than resistance; it calls for pride in who we are and where we come from. To embrace our identity is to embody responsibility and serve as a source of light in a world too often consumed by darkness. We carry the weight of history, but with it comes the power to illuminate a path forward. One firmly rooted in justice, truth, education, innovation, and enduring hope.

Ford Motor Company's response to these tweets was swift but fell short of what the moment demanded. This could have been an opportunity for Ford to lead by example—embracing transparency, taking accountability, and demonstrating an unwavering commitment to its American community. Particularly in a city that has become a hotbed of extremism.

The timing of this incident, just hours before the new year, feels like an opportunity for us all. It's a moment to reassess and reaffirm the values we hold dear—for our families, our communities, and our collective future. As antisemitism continues to seep into the mainstream discourse, our society grows weaker, we become more divided, increasingly intolerant, and more violent. The longer we allow this hatred to take root, the further we drift from the ideals that define the "American Dream." Now is the time for unlearning dangerous narratives and holding individuals and companies accountable, while leading with the principles that have made this nation strong.

CHESS

Can you imagine that lighting a candle to pray, studying Torah, or learning Hebrew could cost you your freedom? In the Soviet Union, these weren't quiet acts of devotion; they were acts of rebellion. I thought of this as I walked down a softly lit alleyway in Jerusalem, the old stone beneath my feet echoing with centuries of memory. At the end of the alley was a dinner that changed me forever: a table set with one of my personal heroes, Natan Sharansky.

Sharansky was more than a dissident. He was the face of the *refusenik* movement, a man who carried the weight of Jewish longing for freedom behind the Iron Curtain.[153]Arrested for wanting to live as a Jew and immigrate to Israel, he spent nine years imprisoned—more than 400 days of that in solitary confinement. His body was broken down to 77 pounds, sleeping on cold floors without heat in brutal Russian winters, with food rations arriving only every other day. His identity was his crime. His Jewishness was his sentence.

And yet, across the dinner table from me in Jerusalem, he radiated humility. He carried no bitterness. Instead, his voice, thick with a Russian accent, was a living archive of history, steady and unflinching. I sat listening to a man who not only survived the unthinkable but went on to become a statesman, an author, a minister in the Knesset, and a global conscience for democracy.[154]

What kept him alive, he told us, were two things. First, chess. A childhood chess prodigy, Sharansky played match after match in his mind, often imagining multiple boards at once.[155] The discipline of strategy, the movement of pieces unseen, kept him sharp when everything around him was designed to break him. Second, a book of Psalms—a wedding gift from his wife, Avital. He recited verses in the darkness, weaving an inner sanctuary when his outer world was stripped bare.

Chess and Psalms: strategy and soul. These unlikely companions gave him freedom in confinement.

That paradox is what makes Sharansky so enduringly relevant. He teaches us that freedom isn't only the absence of bars—it's the presence of clarity, discipline, and faith. And it is this same clarity that carried him from a prison cell to the Knesset. His later achievements read like a statesman's résumé: author of seminal books on democracy and identity, Minister of Industry and Trade, Deputy Prime Minister under Ariel Sharon, recipient of the Congressional Gold Medal, the US Presidential Medal of Freedom, and the Ronald Reagan Freedom Award. But what I find most applicable are not his titles, but his *Three D's*: Delegitimization, Demonization, and Double Standards.[156] These are the markers he used to identify antisemitism, even when it is disguised in casual conversations closer to home.

DARVO

Effective conversations require intention and effort. They demand an openness to truly listen and a willingness to learn. Embedded within the blueprint of the Jewish soul is a tradition of challenging, sharing history, educating ourselves, and growing together. This very ethos was widely championed in 2020, post–George Floyd, a call to listen and learn from those in pain.

It was in that same spirit that I agreed to meet with Tennessee State Representative Aftyn Behn. Just days after October 7th—the deadliest attack on Jews since the Holocaust—she posted a public statement calling for a ceasefire. What was absent from her words was as telling as what she included: no mention of the hostages dragged into Gaza, no recognition of rape being used as a weapon of war, no acknowledgment that Israel was defending its citizens against terrorism. Instead, her language mirrored the talking points of a local BDS organization in Nashville with whom she openly aligned. I wanted to believe that if we sat down face-to-face, away from the curated filters of social media, she might be open to listening, to nuance, to truth.

Natan Sharansky gave me a compass for moments like this. After years of surviving Soviet prisons, he distilled antisemitism into the Three D's framework—Demonization, Double Standards, and Delegitimization. These are the red lines that reveal when criticism of Israel crosses into hatred of Jews. Demonization happens when Israel or Jews are cast as pure evil, compared to Nazis, or stripped of their humanity. Double standards emerge when Israel is judged by rules no other nation is held to, condemned for actions ignored elsewhere. Delegitimization is the most corrosive of all—the denial of Israel's right to exist, the rejection of the Jewish people's right to self-determination. I carried Sharansky's test with me like armor, because without a way to name the patterns, they can overwhelm you in real time.

And as I sat across from Aftyn, I recognized a familiar pattern. DARVO: Deny, Attack, Reverse Victim and Offender[157]—a psychological tactic used to fracture truth, evade accountability, and invert moral clarity. I had first encountered it years earlier while studying the dynamics of emotional abuse, where distortion and manufactured confusion become tools of power and silence. The sensation returned at once: truth turned inside out, responsibility slipped away, and the violent perpetrator recast as the wounded—now pleading innocence.

The setting was strikingly at odds with the conversation itself. We met in the polished back bar of Restoration Hardware in the heart of Nashville, Tennessee. A space defined by upholstered velvet seating, low chandelier lighting, and an atmosphere more befitting her jaunt at the United Nations in Switzerland. Yet in walked Aftyn, wearing a patched jean jacket missing its sleeves—performative rebellion in denim. The contrast set the tone. She ordered champagne.

During our exchange, a few details sharpened the picture. She was young, from a small Southern town, and dating someone nearly twenty years her senior who allegedly is raising a child who identifies as trans.

As the conversation unfolded, the pieces started to fall into place. As I sipped my green tea, it became clearer: her campaign was laser-focused on trans rights. Which raised a larger question: Why was she so eager to wade into the fraught and complex terrain of geopolitics—particularly a conflict so far removed from both her platform and her jurisdiction?

Then it clicked.

Was this the newest face of antisemitism—reshaped to fit the moral language of the moment, thanks to BDS?[158] For the progressive left, old blood libels were being repackaged as social justice claims, their emotional force weaponized through BDS narratives and digital amplification.

For three hours, we sparred across the table. She employed political DARVO; I relied on Sharansky's Three D's. She denied Jewish pain, attacked Israel's legitimacy, denied self-determination, and reversed victim and offender. I countered with history, law, and moral clarity. The exchange was intense and revealing. In the end, her words exposed more than her arguments ever could.

I picked up the bill.

Fast-forward to July 2024 in Music City, USA. Neo-Nazis from the Goyim Defense League paraded past Broadway's honky-tonks, harassed Jewish synagogues, and showed up at a Jewish Federation unity rally—where I encountered them directly. One of them sneered that I was "too pretty to be a Jew" while pressing a flyer into my hand blaming Jews for the world's ills.

Soon after, State Rep. Aftyn Behn seized the moment with both a Substack post[159] and an official letter on state letterhead. She wrote: "It is essential to address the root causes that have led to the rise and confidence of the far-right in our state, exacerbated by the xenophobic, anti-trans, and pro-carceral policies aggressively pushed by the Republican supermajority."

Notably, she never once mentioned Jews, the Holocaust, or even the word "antisemitism." That omission matters.

When someone speaks about Nazis while erasing their central target, it flattens the truth. It rewrites history. And it robs the public of the education we urgently need: that antisemitism is not just "one hate among many." It is the core animating ideology of Nazism—then and now.

And yet, Behn politicized what should be a nonpartisan issue, turning Jewish pain into a stage prop for her platform. Exploiting antisemitism as campaign currency seems to be the newest tactic.

The irony doesn't end there. She condemns Nazis on the far right—but when Iranian-funded encampments appear on college campuses, she cheerleads the spectacle on her X account. When local BDS groups push anti-Israel and antisemitic campaigns, she amplifies them. This convergence is part of what's often called the *Red-Green Alliance*—the strange marriage of the far left ("red") and Islamist movements ("green"), both united in their hostility to Jews and Israel.[160] They come from opposite worldviews, but when it comes to targeting Jews, they find common cause. That's why campus encampments and Nazi marches start to sound like they're reading from the same script.[161]

Someone who lacks this level of critical thinking has no place in public office. Nashville is stronger than this—and our leadership should be, too.

MOBILIZING LIONS

"I am not here to lead sheep; I am here to awaken lions." The words echoed through the small conference room at the King David Hotel in Jerusalem, delivered with the unmistakable conviction of Javier Milei, the president of Argentina. I sat in the front row, an earpiece translating his rapid-fire economic rollout plan into my ear.

Today, his policies are hailed as Argentina's economic miracle, but at that moment, as I absorbed his ambitious vision for sealing a budget surplus, I couldn't help but think: How on earth did I end up here at a press conference as a delegate in Jerusalem? The intricacies of fiscal policy were fascinating, if not fully over my head, but just as my mind began to wander, I glanced to my left.

Wait. No way. Could it be? OMG, yes!

There she was, my Instagram friend and the former deputy mayor of Jerusalem, Fleur Hassan-Nahoum, sitting just two seats down. A familiar face in an unexpected place.

After the conference wrapped, we locked eyes and then exchanged one of those warm hugs that feels like a serendipitous full-circle moment, the kind that reminds you just how small the world can be. Sometimes, the stars really do align. And that day, they did.

Later that afternoon, Fleur invited me to her studio in East Jerusalem, not just as a visitor, but as a guest on her show. Without hesitation, I said yes. My dear friend Alex came along for the adventure. Picture this: a Swedish blonde bombshell with an Egyptian-Jewish father, speaking fluent Hebrew as if she was born to it, standing next to me as we piled into a cab heading straight for the "West Bank." Or, as history honors, Judea and Samaria.

Our Israeli cab driver, a Jewish man with deep lines of caution etched across his face, shot us a knowing look before we stepped out of his rundown car. With a firm but concerned voice, he warned us not to wander the neighborhood. We nodded, took his advice to heart, and slipped inside the guarded gate.

Fleur's studio had an energy all its own, much like the region itself: complex, honest, holy, and tragic all at once. She runs a wildly popular television show called *The Quad* featuring sharp, no-nonsense segments titled "Scumbag of the Week" and "Hero of the Week." In them, she spotlights those who deserve recognition and those who deserve a serious reality check.

It was perfect timing. Just days before, I had been doxed online.

As for my hero? Without hesitation: Natan Sharansky and David Bernstein. Sharansky, a symbol of resilience and Jewish strength, and Bernstein, who courageously called out the dangers of "Woke Antisemitism" and founded the North American Values Institute.

Lights. Camera. Action.

There I was—sitting in a TV studio in Israel, of all places—when, for the first time, I felt seen. Not just for who I was, but for what I'd been shouting into the void for far too long: the staggering rise of antisemitism within my own political party. I've been a registered Democrat my entire life. If you've made it this far into the book—*congratulations*—that might feel like a bit of a plot twist. But these days, I feel politically homeless. Like I showed up to a house I helped build, only to find the locks changed, the lights off, and my mezuzah torn off the doorframe.

Now? I lead with common sense.

As the cameras rolled, I couldn't help but think back to the words of David Bernstein in *Woke Antisemitism*. They jumped off the pages and landed right in my heart. I kept nodding, yes, yes, yes. His message resonated so deeply that I named him my hero of 2024, right then and there on air. David encourages us to connect the dots for others. And I did; I helped illustrate how antisemitism is a shape-shifting mind virus, contorting itself to fit the empty spaces of a society desperate to avoid responsibility.

It's easy to spot antisemitism on the right: swastikas, slurs, and outright hate.[162] But the progressive left? That's where it thrives in disguise. It's woven into the fabric of DEI, CRT, and BDS initiatives, wrapped in the language of justice while violating the very essence of the 1964 Civil Rights Act. These movements, meant to fight discrimination, now actively discriminate against Jews and skin color. It's insidious. It's dangerous. And it's time we called it out.

And so I did. In that small TV studio in East Jerusalem, I spoke up. Because silence wasn't an option anymore.

MOBILIZING FEAR

When I opened the cab door to head back to Tel Aviv from the studio, I felt it instantly—something was off. The driver's eyes locked onto us, dark and calculating, his expression simmering with something between suspicion and anger. My pulse quickened.

Before sliding into the worn back seat, Alex and I instinctively tucked away our Star of David necklaces and hid our hostage bracelets beneath our sleeves. But it didn't matter. He knew. We knew. And in that moment, the weight of where we were hit me like a freight train. It would take just one turn of his wheel, one press of his foot on the accelerator, and we'd be heading straight into Palestinian-occupied territory in the West Bank, aka Judea Samaria, disappearing from the world in an instant. The next time anyone saw us, it would be our faces flashing across CNN or Fox News with headlines we didn't want to imagine.

I gripped the door handle so tight my knuckles turned white, silently calculating how fast I could throw myself from a moving vehicle if it came to that. *Good thing I wore my Converse*, I thought, a ridiculous flash of pragmatism cutting through my panic. These shoes had carried me through all sorts of terrain. Surely, they could outrun this, too, if needed.

The driver's voice cut through the air, sharp and agitated, his tone rising with every sentence. I didn't dare respond. Instead, I sent a text to Alex with fight-or-flight fingers.

"Do we need to get out of this car now?"

She read it, then glanced up at the driver, her body language shifting effortlessly into calm negotiation mode. Alex, with her perfect Hebrew and unshakable composure, started talking, lighthearted, disarming, weaving words like a lifeline. I watched her closely, praying the tension would break. Man, she needs to be negotiating higher stakes.

Seconds felt like hours, and I held my breath until I saw it: the subtle change in his posture, the slow unclenching of his jaw. He wasn't happy, but he was no longer on edge. Alex had done it.

We exhaled in silent relief as the car finally lurched forward, heading in the right direction. Still, my grip never loosened from the door handle until the skyline of Tel Aviv came into view.

P.A.C.E.

A REFLECTIVE + INTERACTIVE DISCUSSION GUIDE FOR BOOK CLUBS

Mobilizing IHRA

P PAUSE

Take a moment to sit with the history you've just read. The Protocols of the Elders of Zion wasn't just a hoax. It is still a current tool of mass political mobilization, designed to turn societies against their Jewish neighbors.

Even though the Protocols was exposed as a forgery over a century ago, its central lie—that Jews secretly control governments, economies, and the media—still echoes today. It's been repackaged and adapted across political movements, from far-right conspiracy theorists to far-left anti-Zionists, from white supremacist forums to Iranian-backed campus protests.

Pause here to reflect:

1. Where do you see these narratives showing up in today's cultural and political climate? Consider protests, online personalities, and even mainstream media.
2. Have you ever heard themes like "globalists," "Zionist cabal," "Jewish Power," or "Jewish money" in conversations, on social media, or in mainstream media?
3. How do these coded conspiracies, sometimes wrapped in language about "the elites," "shadowy forces," or "imperialists," slip into mainstream discourse, often unchallenged?
4. Have you personally encountered antisemitic tropes masked as "anti-corporate," "anti-elite," "anti-imperialist," "decolonizing" or "anti-colonialist" messaging?
5. How have different ideological movements—the far-right through Nazism, the far-left through anti-colonialist activism, and radical Islamism through jihadist propaganda—all

embraced and adapted these conspiracies to suit their own political goals?

6. What does it mean that these seemingly opposing extremes, one preaching racial purity, another revolutionary purity, and others religious or ideological purity, all find common ground in scapegoating Jews?

A ANALYZE

Let's break down what this convergence really looks like.

The far right and far left often claim to stand for opposite values, one obsessed with racial purity, the other with dismantling systems of power. Yet when it comes to Jews, they converge, united by the same old lies, conspiracies, and masks to hide their true intentions.

- The far right frames Jews as disloyal, rootless globalists, a threat to racial purity, Christian identity, and nationalist ideals. They revive centuries-old antisemitic tropes, casting Jews as secret puppetmasters manipulating immigration, banking, and culture.
- The far left rebrands antisemitism as anti-colonialism and anticapitalism, portraying Jews as colonial settlers, imperialist aggressors, and financial elites hoarding wealth at the expense of the oppressed. They frame Jews as the ultimate beneficiaries of white privilege, erasing the reality of Jewish persecution and displacement.
- Both sides, despite their opposing rhetoric, use Jews as a convenient scapegoat, blamed for economic collapse, social unrest, war, and even the failures of their own ideologies.

Show me the cultural crisis, and I will show you how you blame the Jews.

Both mask their ideologies:

- The far right might wear white hoods or neo-Nazi insignia.

- The far left might don white keffiyehs, presenting themselves as anti-colonial freedom fighters.
- But at their core, both are supremacist movements, seeing Jews as the ultimate enemy—the symbol of everything they claim to fight against.

C CONTEMPLATE

Take a moment to reflect on the power of defining and recognizing antisemitism in today's world.

1. Has your state adopted the International Holocaust Remembrance Alliance (IHRA) definition of antisemitism? This definition, established in 2016, serves as a crucial tool for identifying antisemitism in all its forms. From historical prejudice to modern expressions, like the delegitimization of Israel or the denial of the Holocaust, it provides a clear framework for understanding and confronting hatred. It has already been adopted by many countries, universities, organizations, and government institutions as a resource to educate about and fight against antisemitism.
2. If your state has adopted this definition, take the opportunity to call your legislators and thank them for their support. It's a small but meaningful way to show gratitude for their commitment to combating hatred and promoting inclusivity.
3. If not, it's time to . . .

E ENGAGE

Now that you've reflected on the significance of a shared definition, it's time to take concrete steps toward making a difference.

Reach Out to Your Community. Start by talking to friends, family, and colleagues about the importance of adopting the IHRA working definition of antisemitism. Share what you've learned and encourage others to get involved. The more people understand the issue, the stronger the collective impact.[163]

Get Involved in Local Advocacy. Join or support groups that are working to educate about antisemitism and push for policy changes at the state and national levels. Advocate for your state to adopt the IHRA definition if it hasn't already, and help raise awareness in your local community.

Hold Public Officials Accountable. If your state hasn't adopted the IHRA definition, reach out to your local legislators. Share your concerns, explain why the definition is crucial, and encourage them to support it. Stay engaged and follow up with them to ensure that this important issue remains on the agenda.

Amplify the Conversation. Use social media to share resources, articles, and information about antisemitism and the IHRA definition. Help spread the message and keep the conversation going. The more we engage, the more we can create lasting change.

Your involvement matters. By taking these steps, you're not just speaking up; you're helping create a culture where antisemitism is recognized and rejected at every level.

CHAPTER 10

BDS IN YOUR BACKYARD

Mid-morning found me on the kitchen floor, wrestling with an overstuffed suitcase. I was heading back to Israel as a delegate with the American Jewish Committee. But this wasn't just a quick trip; I extended my stay to visit Judea and Samaria with council member and rabbi Yishai Fleisher, and I had meetings lined up at the Knesset and with the new deputy mayor of Jerusalem.

I pressed down hard, praying the zipper would hold. With a small, triumphant grunt, it finally did. Small win.

It was sweltering. The kind of sticky Southern summer heat that clings like a second skin.

I threw my suitcase in the car. My hair matted to my face, as the air-conditioning struggled against the relentless humidity that seeped deep into my bones.

At the airport, I approached the counter and handed over my suitcase and credit card without hesitation, already bracing for the charge. The woman behind the desk barely glanced at the scale before sliding over my receipt.

"Where are you headed?" she asked, her voice polite with indifference.

"Newark, then Israel," I said quietly.

Her eyes flicked up to meet mine, softening with concern.

"Be safe," she said genuinely.

I nodded, absorbing the weight of her words with a smile, and headed toward security. Miraculously, I breezed through, no TSA pat-downs, no frantic rummaging through my carefully packed belongings.

Ding.

Ding.

Ding.

My phone started pinging incessantly. I glanced at the screen just as the announcement blared overhead: my flight was delayed.

Fantastic.

I started mentally troubleshooting worst-case scenarios—missed connections, re-bookings, scrambling to find another flight. But it's not that easy when you are flying into a war zone.

It was June 2024 and El Al was the only airline still flying into Tel Aviv, and honestly, it's the only one I trust. Considered one of the world's most secure airlines, El Al is equipped with anti-missile defense systems that protect against surface-to-air missiles. Yes, because this is what happens when genocidal psychopaths in a ring of fire target innocent civilians on land and in air.

I was juggling my phone, my luggage, my hot coffee, and trying to get from point A to B. One step closer to seeing, in the palm of my hand, what war was erupting or what fire needed putting out because, well, it all started last week . . . on a Sunday . . . on an ascending escalator in the mall.

My phone had buzzed with a PDF, a Resolution RS2024-556 being floated at Nashville Metro Council. At first glance, the document detonated a cascade of questions and serious next steps, colliding with my mundane plans to finish packing and take a lighthearted trip to the mall. By Monday morning, the resolution had felt manageable. I dove head in. I was on with a trusted mentor, a retired attorney and lobbyist whose reputation preceded her. She had played a pivotal role in codifying Tennessee's anti-BDS bill in 2022 and had spearheaded the state's adoption of the International Holocaust Remembrance Alliance (IHRA) definition of antisemitism.[164] During our call, she unraveled the complexities of Tennessee politics with razor-sharp clarity, while I googled key phrases from the document, and then, there it was. I froze.

This wasn't just another local legislative document.

It was a Trojan horse.

The "ceasefire resolution" was sponsored by Muslim Nigerian-born Metro Council Member-at-Large Zulfat Suara[165] (who also co-founded the American Muslim Advisory Council, an ally of the Council on American-Islamic Relations).[166] The language, structure, and talking points of the resolution were a copy-paste job lifted directly from a toolkit published by the US Campaign for Palestinian Rights (USCPR)—the largest umbrella organization of over 300 BDS groups in North America (formerly named End the Israeli Occupation). These are the very groups across the country that have been inciting violence, vandalism, and anti-Western rhetoric while parroting slogans of terrorist regimes. I had never seen anything like it before: hundreds of links to Google Drive toolkit after toolkit after toolkit after toolkit, with this one in particular packed with sixteen pages, outlining where to begin, to whom to apply pressure, whom to publicly shame, which groups to target, how to exploit guilt, how to notify newsrooms, how to print propaganda, how to act like an "American," and how to avoid being doxxed.

I knew what I was holding. And I knew how quickly it could slip through without a fight.

By Monday afternoon, I filmed a reel exposing the truth and I cleared my calendar. Hours of nonstop calls followed—community leaders, attorneys, council members, donors—each conversation was another hand linked into a chain, strengthening our resolve. There was no time for fatigue. This wasn't just about one city's resolution; it was about the machinery behind it, the playbook designed to delegitimize Israel by planting falsehoods on American soil.

Then came Tuesday. The timing felt almost divine. On short notice, I was asked to moderate an event with Holocaust survivor Joe Alexander. Joe is 101 years old. He survived twelve concentration camps and a death march. But the extraordinary thing about Joe isn't just what he endured—it's what he built afterward. A family, a business, a community. He didn't speak with bitterness. He didn't dramatize. His authority came from the simple fact of his presence: living proof that human dignity does outlast evil. He lived his life as a rebuttal to the idea that hatred wins. For me, it was an essential reminder: surviving hatred is only part of the story. The greater victory is learning to thrive beyond it.

As he spoke next to me on the bimah, I thought about the resolution I spent all day fighting the day before. About how before there are camps, there are boycotts. Before there are broken bodies, there are broken truths. Joe's story wasn't just history. It was instruction. A reminder that the same seeds that once led to genocide were being scattered again—this time, with Google Drive toolkits and metro city council agendas.

By Wednesday, the resolution was withdrawn. A small but decisive victory. Not because one person shouted the loudest, but because a community linked arms and we said "NO."

And then came Friday.

At the gate, I sat down, inhaled, exhaled. My now-lukewarm coffee sat untouched beside me. I unlocked my phone, scrolling through the messages waiting for me. For a moment, I just stared. Then a smile crept across my face. Not out of arrogance, not even defiance. But because I thought of Joe. A man who had endured the worst of humanity and still chose to rebuild, to teach, to lead by living.

If being called and linked as a "vocal critic or a social media troll" in an opinion piece by David Plazas in *The Tennessean* was the price of carrying that torch forward—of standing between poisoned words and the people they could harm—then so be it.

Words matter, and so does context. Plazas's op-ed was not neutral. It echoed the very biases embedded in the resolution itself. By framing Jewish voices, like mine, as "trolls," he dismissed legitimate concerns as noise. By repeating the language of "Israel and Palestine," he falls into a false equivalence trap. The local "resolution" referred to "Israel and Palestine," implying a parity that simply does not exist. Israel has been a recognized state by the United States since 1948. "Palestine" as a state has never existed. Not in history, not in international law—yet this language is a revisionist attempt from a group that openly seeks Israel's destruction and does not recognize it as a state. Additionally, he omitted the resolution's direct ties to the US Campaign for Palestinian Rights—the largest BDS umbrella organization in North America whose goal is to delegitimize the State of Israel economically, socially, and academically. He uncritically quoted Suara's description of the resolution as a "peace bill," conveniently ignoring the fact that there *was* peace—until October 7th, when Hamas shattered it with a barbaric assault on Israeli civilians. The tragic loss of life on both sides stems directly from Hamas's aggression, not Israel's defense. Finally, he leaned on selective statistics about Islamophobia while ignoring the FBI's own data that Jews are the most targeted religious group in America. The resolution cites "Islamophobia" statistics directly from the Council on American-Islamic Relations (CAIR), an organization with well-documented ties to Hamas. Watchdog Canary Mission exposed CAIR's connections to terrorism, incitement, and BDS with links to terror financiers.[167]

Clarity matters.

Leadership is not about yielding to the trends, but about standing in truth when the cost of our silence is too high. If we want stronger communities—and stronger leaders—we must refuse to be lulled by bullshit platitudes that mask destructive agendas. Because what happened in Nashville was not an isolated resolution. It was the local face of a much larger campaign.

BDS IS THE NEW INTIFADA

I've mentioned BDS in previous chapters. Let's get into it.

BDS: A Sleeper Cell for Domestic Terror

The Boycott, Divestment, and Sanctions (BDS) movement might seem like a distant geopolitical issue to many, but its destruction is creeping into our own local communities. While it presents itself as a peaceful, nonviolent campaign aimed at helping "Palestinians," it's baloney and functions as the "diplomatic" arm for organizations that promote violence and terrorism. Supporting BDS means not just targeting Israel. It means you're supporting a dangerous narrative that prioritizes terrorist ideologies over our Western values.

What Is BDS?

Think of the BDS movement as a team sport for terrorism. Their team chants in recent years have been "From the River to the Sea" and "Allahu Akbar," with the sole goal of eradicating and delegitimizing the State of Israel. Like any team, they have a coach, players, and a home field. The coach is Omar Barghouti, who solidified the movement in 2005, building on its conception during a pre-meeting in Tehran in 2001, just before the UN-sponsored Durban Conference in South Africa.[168]

The Durban Conference set the stage for this "team," bringing together nations and organizations, many with their own histories of human rights violations, under the banner of combating "racism." Instead, it became a breeding ground for anti-Israel and anti-Jewish sentiment. NGOs at Durban labeled Israel as an "apartheid state"[169] and called for its isolation using the very tactics now championed by BDS.[170]

The playbook wasn't new. It borrowed heavily from Soviet-era propaganda, which weaponized anti-Zionism as a cover for antisemitism during the Cold War.[171] The Soviet Union framed Israel as a colonial, racist enterprise to align with its geopolitical strategy of courting Arab nations. This disinformation laid the groundwork for BDS, whose goal is to repurpose these tactics into a globalized strategy to isolate and weaken Israel politically, economically, and socially.

With every movement comes players and supporters who take the field. The BDS "team" includes NGOs, political figures, and activists; student groups and even institutions have adopted its rhetoric under the guise of social justice.[172]

Their "home field" is wherever these ideas can infiltrate, be it international conferences, college campuses, or city councils (hello, Zulfat Suara and Aftyn Behn, we see you), turning communities into battlegrounds for a domestic terrorist ideology.

BDS CLAIM VERSUS REALITY

The Boycott, Divestment, and Sanctions movement outlines three primary goals, presenting them as calls for "human rights and justice." However, I urge all critical thinkers to approach BDS with a healthy dose of skepticism, as its objectives quickly crumble under closer scrutiny. Let's not forget: any "social justice" that steps on the neck of another just makes you a bully.

ONE: End Israel's "Occupation and Colonization of all Arab Lands" and Dismantle the Security Barrier.

The Claim: BDS asserts that Israel is an "occupying" power, framing the presence of Jews in Judea and Samaria (the "West Bank") and the Gaza Strip as colonization. They demand a complete withdrawal from these territories, labeling the security barrier as a symbol of "apartheid."

The Reality: A Misrepresentation of "Occupation." The term "occupation" is weaponized to delegitimize Israel's existence, and our indigeneity. BDS co-founder Omar Barghouti admitted, "We oppose a Jewish state in any part of Palestine." This statement reveals that the movement's true goal is dismantling Israel, not reforming its policies or having peaceful coexistence.[173]

Cliff Notes Context: Israel gained control of Judea and Samaria during the 1967 Six-Day War,[174] a purely defensive war against attacks from its Arab neighbors, including Egypt's closure of the Straits of Tiran and the mobilization of Arab armies. Rather than colonizing, Israel sought "land for peace," offering to return territories in exchange for peace agreements, which Arab nations rejected under the Khartoum Resolution, or the "Three no's": no peace, no recognition, no negotiations with Israel.[175]

Despite these challenges, Israel has successfully signed peace treaties with Egypt (1979) and Jordan (1994). Israel also disengaged from Gaza in 2005, removing Jewish bodies from graves along with military presence.[176]

Security Barrier Saves Lives. The security barrier, built during the Second Intifada, was designed to prevent terrorist attacks targeting Israeli civilians. Suicide bombings, shootings, and stabbings decreased by 90 percent after its construction. While BDS labels it an "apartheid wall," this ignores its role as a life-saving measure. Press outlets are not sounding the alarm or accusing Egypt of apartheid for fortifying its borders with a seven-layered wall system to prevent Palestinians/Gazans from entering. No outrage, no condemnations, as Egypt rightfully protects its civilians just as Israel has done.[177]

Furthermore, organizations such as Palestinian Media Watch have documented financial incentives provided by the Palestinian Authority to families of terrorists who kill and/or stab Jews and Israelis, a practice often referred to as "pay-for-slay," or what I like to call it: subsidized slaughter (hence, walls and checkpoints are necessary).

Pay for Slay: A finely tuned economic machine where murder isn't just encouraged, it's incentivized, structured, and systematically rewarded.[178] Call it terror wages, blood bounties, murder-for-money, death dividends, or an extremist compensation scheme. Whatever the label, the business model stays the same. I don't say this casually. I speak with deep sensitivity for the countless victims of this level of evil. In the

West, we are largely shielded from such depravity, making it difficult to fully grasp. For that reason, I will be discussing it with a little wit and in terms we can understand.

Think multi-level marketing for murders—your new MLMM. A pyramid scheme of terror where the buy-in is a stabbing in Jerusalem, and the payouts never stop. The West is fixated on influencer marketing? Well, here's the terrorist version, a martyrdom rewards program. Like it? Now fund it. Call it Profit-Driven Martyrdom™. A one-way express pass to paradise, complete with a fantasy-package of 9,000 virgins. And who's running the books? The PLO—your friendly neighborhood Blood Money Brokerage, making sure every transaction of terror gets its proper payout.[179]

Here's the slaughter sliding scale, with the monthly salary in Israeli shekels:[180]

- 1,400 shekels (USD 383.90): paid to a father who knew his son was planning an attack on the Barkan Industrial Park and did not report it. Two were killed.
- 2,000 shekels (USD 548.43): paid to a terrorist who threw stones at an Israeli vehicle, injuring an infant.
- 4,000 shekels (USD 1,090.00): paid to a terrorist who threw a Molotov cocktail at a car, injuring two.
- 6,000 shekels (USD 1,645.30): paid to a terrorist who stabbed a twelve-year-old, inflicting near fatal injury.
- 7,000 shekels (USD 1,919.52): paid to a terrorist who supplied weapons to conduct surveillance, and another terrorist who murdered an Israeli hiker.
- 8,000 shekels (USD 2,193.74): paid to a terrorist who ran over and injured twelve IDF soldiers.
- 10,000 shekels (USD 2,742.17): paid to a terrorist who murdered a couple in front of their small children.
- 12,000 shekels (USD 3,290.61): paid to a terrorist who murdered the couple Rabbi Eitam and Naama Henkin in front of their small children.

Source: Lital Shemesh, "How much is a dead Jew worth?" *Tablet* magazine, February 26, 2025.

According to Gideon Sa'ar, foreign affairs minister of Israel: "The Palestinian Authority hasn't stopped its payments of salaries to terrorists and their families. In fact, it is nearly doubling them. In 2024, it paid $144 million (€124 million). In 2025, it has already committed $214 million (€185 million) toward Pay-for-Slay, and the year isn't even over."[181]

This is a system that reduces human lives to commodities, traded on a scale that doesn't measure the worth of life but the level of terror inflicted. The more brutal the act, the higher the price tag. This scale ensures that the most aggressive, the most heinous violations, are the ones that bring the highest rewards. It's a chilling, calculated system where brutality becomes the currency, a game of price tags that only grows with the escalating bloodshed that has been unrelenting for decades.

To put this into perspective, Holocaust survivor Ludmila Lipovsky, at eighty-three years old, was waiting for her daughter to take her to a doctor's appointment when a twenty-eight-year-old Palestinian man stabbed her to death.[182] After surviving the horrors of the Holocaust, she tragically met her end at the hands of those who still carry the same genocidal ideology as the Nazis.[183] Since her death in December 2024, the number of similar incidents has only multiplied—too many to count.

Each one is a haunting reminder of how history's darkest shadows continue to plague the present.

Meanwhile, the lives of Palestinians are often valued more in prison, where their families are provided with housing and care, transforming violence into a twisted form of support, an incentive that perpetuates the cycle of hatred. To those who are adamant about freeing Palestinians, I urge you to start by freeing them from the very ideologies that keep them shackled and oppressed, preventing them from breaking free and forging a future of peace, prosperity, and dignity.

Legal Rights to the Land. Israel's claims to Judea and Samaria are grounded in international law, including the 1920 San Remo Resolution and the League of Nations Mandate for Palestine, which recognized

Jewish rights to establish a homeland in these territories.[184] The deliberate omission of these precedents by BDS aims to delegitimize Israel's historical and legal connection to the land.

The Only Thing "Occupied" Is Terror over Peace. Israel has made multiple offers for a Palestinian state. For instance, in 2008, then–Prime Minister Ehud Olmert proposed withdrawing from 93 percent of Judea and Samaria, along with land swaps, to establish a Palestinian state.[185] The offer was rejected by Palestinian leadership. Both the Palestinian Authority and Hamas continue to prioritize terror and propaganda over the well-being of their people, perpetuating the conflict.[186]

TWO: Recognize the Rights of Arab-Palestinian Citizens of Israel to Full Equality.

The Claim: BDS portrays Israel as an "apartheid state," alleging systemic discrimination against Arab citizens, and demands "full equality."

The Reality: Equal Rights Under the Law.

Arab citizens of Israel, who make up about 20 percent of the population, are granted full citizenship and the same legal rights as Jewish citizens. They can vote, run for office, and are represented in the Knesset (Israeli parliament).[187] Notably, Arab citizens serve in high-ranking roles, such as in the judiciary, where Judge Salim Joubran, an Arab, served on the Israeli Supreme Court.[188] This political participation is in stark contrast to apartheid regimes, which deny political rights to nondominant ethnic groups and restrict voting. Arab citizens also benefit from Israel's democratic institutions,[189] such as freedom of speech and religion.[190]

Additionally, Israeli Arab women enjoy greater economic freedom, equality, and educational opportunities than women in any Arab country.[191] Let that sink in: while Israeli Arab women thrive in education and exercise their freedoms in Israel,[192] countries like Afghanistan impose draconian laws banning women from speaking or singing in public, restricting education beyond the age of thirteen, and even forbidding them from standing near windows in their own homes.[193]

Comparison with South African Apartheid: The accusation that Israel is comparable to South Africa's apartheid regime is absurd and ignores Israel's democratic values, diversity, and legal commitment to equality. Apartheid in South Africa enforced systemic racial segregation through laws designed to oppress and marginalize non-white citizens. Non-white citizens were denied voting rights, political representation, interracial marriage, and access to decision-making processes.

Israel by contrast, is a democratic state where Arab citizens have full rights and actively participate in society. Groups like BDS misuse the term "apartheid" to delegitimize Israel's existence.[194]

In Israel public spaces, including hospitals, schools, and transportation, are shared by all citizens.[195] Road signs, airport signs, and public transport signs are written in Hebrew, Arabic, and English, reflecting the country's inclusivity and linguistic diversity.[196]

In Israel, the Israeli Declaration of Independence guarantees equal rights to all citizens, regardless of race, religion, or ethnicity. Discrimination is prohibited under Israeli law, and government programs actively aim to reduce socioeconomic disparities in Arab-majority communities.

Additionally, Arab citizens can voluntarily serve in the Israel Defense Forces (IDF) and hold prominent positions in academia, government, and the private sector. One visible example is Captain Ella Waweya, a Muslim Arab Israeli officer who became a recognizable voice across the Arab world. For seven years, she led the IDF's Arabic-language platform known as "Captain Ella," speaking directly to Arab audiences and breaking through layers of misinformation. Her work earned the trust of Israel's highest leadership, including praise from the president, defense minister, and chief of staff. In 2024, she was selected to succeed Avichay Adraee as the IDF's Arabic-language spokesperson after his eighteen-year tenure—an appointment that quietly reflects a reality many prefer to ignore.[197]

Equating Israel with apartheid diminishes the lived experiences of South Africans, and is profoundly insensitive.

THREE: Promote the "Right of Return" for Palestinian Refugees and their Descendants.

The Claim: BDS insists on the "right of return" for millions of Palestinian "refugees" and their descendants, like Bella Hadid. The "right of return" is a political weapon, not a humanitarian call, designed to erase Israel's Jewish identity. The perpetuation of Palestinian refugee status by UNRWA and Arab nations undermines efforts for genuine peace, contrasting with Israel's successful integration of Jewish refugees from Arab countries.

The Reality: A Demographic Weapon. The demand for the "right of return" is not about coexistence but aims to dissolve Israel's Jewish-majority state through a demographic shift. By flooding Israel with millions of descendants claiming expiration-free refugee status, the country's Jewish identity would be erased, undermining its foundation as a state for Jewish people following centuries of persecution.[198]

The United Nations Relief and Works Agency (UNRWA) strategically defines Palestinian refugees to include descendants indefinitely, unlike any other refugee group worldwide. This has inflated the number of refugees from approximately 700,000 in 1948 to over 5.9 million today. No other refugee population retains this hereditary status, making the Palestinian refugee issue an anomaly in international law and policy.[199]

Historical Context of Displacement. The Palestinian refugee crisis originated during the 1948 Arab-Israeli War, when Arab nations invaded Israel after rejecting the UN Partition Plan. Many Palestinians fled due to the war or were encouraged to leave by Arab leaders who promised a swift victory. Meanwhile, approximately 850,000 Jews were expelled from Arab countries in the same period. Unlike Palestinians, these Jewish refugees were fully absorbed by Israel, while Arab nations refused to integrate Palestinians, perpetuating their statelessness for political leverage.[200]

Double Standards in Refugee Policy Unique Refugee Definition. BDS's promotion of the "right of return" ignores that resolving refugee crises typically involves resettlement or integration, not the indefinite maintenance of refugee status. Arab states' refusal to grant citizenship or rights to Palestinian refugees, despite decades of hosting them, exposes the political motives behind this demand.[201]

Shapeshifting Swords Through International Lawfare. The BDS movement employs "lawfare" as a strategic weapon, distorting international legal frameworks to accuse Israel of "apartheid," "colonialism," "genocide," and being a "settler state." These allegations, designed to delegitimize Israel, rely on distorted parallels to South Africa's apartheid regime and misrepresentation of historical and legal facts.[202]

Colonialism and Settler-State Allegations. These accusations ignore the historical and legal context of Israel's establishment. The Jewish connection to the land of Judea spans over 3,000 years, and modern Israel's creation was rooted in the self-determination of an indigenous people returning to their homeland.

The establishment was also sanctioned by international agreements, including the 1922 League of Nations Mandate and the UN Partition Plan of 1947.[203] Israel's existence cannot be equated with colonialism, which typically involves a foreign power exploiting distant lands. By 2023, over 70 percent of Israel's population comprises Jews with roots in the Middle East and North Africa, refuting the settler-colonial narrative.[204] You cannot colonize a land you're indigenous to.

Genocide Claims. The charge of genocide collapses the moment it is tested against reality. By international law, genocide requires both intent and action to destroy (in whole or part) a designated group[205]—a threshold Israel does not meet. As John Spencer, the world's foremost expert in urban warfare, explains, Israel's conduct in Gaza does not reflect indiscriminate violence, but an unprecedented commitment to protecting civilian life in one of the most complex and unforgiving urban battle environments in history. In modern urban war, Spencer notes, civilian casualties rise as density increases. And yet, Israel's combatant-to-civilian casualty ratio is historically low, far below what he notes in major urban battles in Manila, Seoul, or Mosul.[206] This is not accidental. It is the result of a moral, ethical, law-abiding army executing extreme operational restraint to protect civilians. What does that mean? It means offering advance evacuation warnings; humanitarian pauses; millions of leaflets, texts, and phone calls; delayed and aborted strikes; pauses in fighting to administer polio vaccines to the enemy population;[207] and, as confirmed in the UN's Convention on the Prevention and Punishment of the Crime of Genocide (COGAT) December 2025 IPC report,[208] the delivery of over two million tons of humanitarian aid.[209] Even when viewed through Hamas's own deeply flawed numbers, the data simply does not support claims of indiscriminate warfare—let alone genocide. It tells a very different story: of a military bending itself, again and again, toward the preservation of life, while facing an enemy that deliberately embeds itself inside, behind, and underneath its own civilians.

This is what happens when emotion becomes the objective, then numbers become the easiest weapon. Hamas folds every death—whether a combatant, civilian, accidental, or natural death—into a single narrative to artificially inflate its numbers. They blur every line on purpose, launching missiles from schools, mosques, and hospitals, storing weapons in homes, and building tunnels beneath neighborhoods. What results and travels across our screens isn't human rights advocacy. It's narrative laundering and fiction at best.

Just as genocide has a legal definition, it also has an origin—and both matter. The term was coined in 1944 by Polish-Jewish jurist Raphael Lemkin, combining *genos* (race or tribe) and *cide* (killing) to describe the systematic annihilation of Jews during the Holocaust and to ensure that such crimes could never again hide behind legal vagueness.[210] To now hurl this word at the Jewish state—while severing it from both its legal meaning and its historical soul—is not just dishonest. It is an inversion of truth. It turns victims into perpetrators. It transforms moral language into weapons. And in doing so, it drains genocide of its meaning, its gravity, its specificity, and its warning to societies.

Legal Warfare and Manipulation: BDS's accusations are not aimed at fostering coexistence but at undermining Israel's legitimacy. By distorting international law, the movement transforms legal principles into weapons against the only democracy in the Middle East, a nation that guarantees freedom of speech, religion, and assembly for all its citizens. This manipulative approach erodes the foundations of truth and fairness in global diplomacy, echoing Natan Sharansky's observation in *The Free Press* that "international forums have been weaponized against Israel to distort its reality and history."[211]

HERE'S HOW BDS IS IMPACTING OUR DAILY LIVES

Local Governments

Across the United States, city councils and state legislatures have attempted or passed resolutions aligned with BDS rhetoric.

In 2014 in Berkeley, California, a resolution was passed urging divestment from companies tied to Israel. In Seattle and New York, similar pushes to frame boycotts as human rights initiatives alienated Jewish residents.[212]

There has been legislative pushback with select states passing anti-BDS laws, but the movement persists, influencing local discourse and sowing division.

Birds of a feather, radicalize together. In a *New York Post* exclusive, rabid antisemite and BDS super spreader Linda Sarsour was pulling the strings to propel socialist Zohran Mamdani toward becoming New York City's next mayor.

Rich Calder, a political reporter at the same newspaper, captured the concern of the Jewish community in the Big Apple before it rots:

> Hank Sheinkopf, a longtime Democratic consultant, said Sarsour and the rest of the "anti-Israel far left" see Mamdani as a "great opportunity" to seize control of America's largest city.
>
> "This is their moment to try and capture the city's government and turn it into what they want, which is less about

> progressive politics and more about Jew-hating than anything else," said Sheinkopf, who is Jewish.[213]
>
> "Linda Sarsour is not running him because he's a great progressive and believes in some kind of redistribution of wealth. She's running him because he's a great antisemite."

Linda Sarsour, who was born and raised in New York, and has been publicly quoted as saying "nothing is creepier than Zionism," is just one of the many spiders spinning lies in this BDS Charlotte's Web. What do Zulfat Suara, Rashida Tlaib, Tamika Mallory, Justin Jones, Louis Farrakhan, Subhi Ali, Hisham Sharabi, Yousef Munayyer, Ahmad Abuznaid, and Ash-Lee Woodard Henderson all have in common? They are ideological foot soldiers for BDS, with deep roots in Nashville, Tennessee, and a direct pipeline to the Jerusalem Fund and the US Campaign for Palestinian Rights—both of which operate as ideological arms of modern-day ideological terrorism and tax-exempt fronts funneling resources to jihadist networks like Hamas. The alarm isn't just ringing, it's blaring.

Sarsour stepped down as a former co-chair of the Women's March, after repeatedly refusing to fully denounce Louis Farrakhan—who called Jews "termites" in the "Synagogue of Satan"—alongside her cohort Tamika Mallory.

I encourage you to go down the rabbit hole and see how jihadism is taking root in Tennessee, and how it could soon impact your local politics. A great resource is DailyRollCall.com, run by a retired FBI agent who has been tracking this infiltration for years. The connections are deeper than you think.

Schools: A Hotbed for BDS Activism

Ah, the real nightmare isn't a child returning home from college with a tree-hugger's mentality. It's them coming back sporting a homegrown green headband, a symbol of Hamas or the Houthis, proudly worn as their brain cells get hijacked by Qatari-funded departments. While you're thinking they'll be folding their laundry, they're advertising the Third Intifada at your local Whole Foods, ready to preach the very ideology that fuels violence, hate, and extremism.

This is about indoctrination at its finest, subtly disguised as activism but rooted in something far darker. Universities, which once stood as institutions of critical thinking and veritas, are now incubators for dangerous propaganda. The next generation is coming out not with an open mind, but a closed one, groomed for a jihadist agenda funded by the very money that thrives off the destruction of America.

As Canary Mission points out, Columbia University's chapter of Students for Justice in Palestine (SJP) aligned themselves with Hamas's agenda and the destruction of Israel and the United States, all under the guise of fighting for "justice." They linked "anti-Israel" rhetoric with "racial social justice," "climate justice," "gender equality," and more within widely disseminated toolkits pushing their agenda under the banners of "anti-racism" and "anti-war." By doing so, SJP cultivated alliances that reached their peak during the 2020 George Floyd protests and the BLM movement, where chapters across the US didn't just oppose "police states;" they leveraged the moment to specifically and artificially manufacture "Black-Palestinian solidarity."[214]

This is a calculated effort to conflate multiple causes for one anti-American destructive agenda with direct alleged ties to Hamas.

In March 2025 families of Israeli hostages filed a lawsuit in a Manhattan federal court against Columbia's SJP for allegedly "aiding and abetting Hamas's continuing acts of international terrorism." The families cite an Instagram post from SJP that was published THREE MINUTES before Hamas attacked Israel. The account, which was previously dormant, was reactivated on October 5th, 2023—two days before the massacre.[215]

It's not far-fetched to observe that the timing of these posts and reactivation means that there were people in the United States who knew the massacre was scheduled for October 7th, which should make any decent human being sick to their stomach. What we saw on college campuses has a direct link to Hamas through networks such as American Muslims for Palestine (AMP), Students for Justice in Palestine, Within Our Lifetime, Palestinian Youth Movement, The People's Forum, Act Now to Stop War and End Racism (ANSWER), and Jewish Voice for Peace.[216]

The campaign had real implications. Between 2022 and 2025, more than twenty BDS resolutions passed at US universities, and those numbers are growing exponentially.

These were organized, structured, tactical and well-funded encampments. Everyone had their organized jihadi toolkit ripe with green tents, green headbands, posters, markers, sunscreen, and keffiyehs.

And don't even get me started on the Harvard Law School votes to endorse BDS in 2024 and 2025. This wasn't just any vote on an international issue—it was specifically about Israel. The Harvard Law School Alliance for Israel stood firm against it, calling the vote "plainly discriminatory" for singling out the Jewish state. BDS isn't about peace or justice; it's about erasing Israel's right to exist.

American-Jewish Harvard Divinity school graduate Shabbos Kestenbaum was part of the lawsuit against Harvard. On March 14th, 2025, he wrote on X:

> Today, the Harvard Law school student body (72%) voted to boycott, divest, and sanction Israel. The Harvard Law school voted last year to do the same thing. No other international issue has ever been voted on.[217]
>
> The Harvard Law School Alliance for Israel blasted the vote as "plainly discriminatory" and singling out the Jewish state.
>
> I encourage major law firms like Davis Polk that deal extensively in Israel to no longer hire students that voted in favor of boycotting Israel as we wouldn't want these students to compromise their values in exchange for a career.

This latest vote at Harvard is not an isolated event. It's part of a broader, deeply entrenched campaign to delegitimize Israel within American academia. And it's not just about student "activism;" it's about the systemic embrace of a terrorist ideology that openly calls for Israel's destruction.[218]

Additionally, consider Omar Barghouti, the founder of BDS, a man banned from entering the US in 2019, yet who somehow still managed to complete a master's degree at Columbia University.[219] This raises a glaring question: If the very architect of BDS is considered a national security risk, why are we letting the ideology spread like a viral infection across our campuses? It's a rhetorical question, but one that demands an answer.

Social Media BDS

Social media has become a battleground where BDS rhetoric is amplified and normalized, often devoid of context or factual accuracy. Viral campaigns like #fromtherivertothesea, #BDS, and #FreePalestine perpetuate anti-Israel propaganda, reducing complex geopolitical issues to simplistic narratives that vilify Israel. Online voices like Bella Hadid, Amanda Seales, Ericka Hart, and Glennon Doyle use their massive platforms to echo BDS talking points. This isn't just "sharing an opinion"—it's shaping public perception. By demonizing Israel while erasing the reality of terrorism, they fuel narratives that translate into real-world hostility toward Jewish communities. The cost is steep. For Jewish voices online, even a single post in support of Israel can unleash harassment, death threats, career risks, and social isolation.

Workplace BDS

BDS has extended its influence into workplaces, creating divisive and often toxic environments. Activist employees at major corporations like Google and Amazon have pushed for divestment from Israel, fostering tension and pressuring colleagues to align with their political stance. In the public sector, similar pressures emerge as government institutions are increasingly drawn into BDS campaigns, forcing employees to take sides on complex geopolitical issues. These dynamics not only polarize professional spaces but also marginalize those who support Israel, making it difficult to maintain neutrality or foster inclusivity in the workplace.

Book Publishing

The Gaza war has become a war on Jewish books and authors. I personally experienced this when I lost a significant book deal after sharing my support for Israel and for pushing back by educating against antisemitism. This escalating climate of hostility doesn't just silence Jewish authors. It actively erases our stories, attempting to render us invisible. The antidote? Writing more, publishing more, and building spaces where our voices refuse to be ignored.

My friend, writing peer, and publisher, Zibby Owens, understood this urgency and created the anthology *On Being Jewish Now*, a literary refuge for those of us who found ourselves losing publishing deals, uninvited from stages, and erased from conferences. In a time when truth comes at a cost, this book stands as both defiance and a declaration: We are still here, and our stories will be told. And this very book you are holding? Consider it my unapologetic middle finger to a publishing industry still asleep at the wheel—blind to the rising tide of Jew-hatred, much of it fueled straight from Tehran.

Here's a snapshot of what it was like for Jewish authors in 2024:

On March 3rd, 2024, the *Telegraph* reported that half of British publishers were refusing to publish books by authors who were "identifiably Jewish."[220]

Later that spring, on May 10th, 2024, a Google spreadsheet titled "Is your favorite author a Zionist?" went viral for collecting names of authors who were simply Jewish, which led to a boycott of more Jewish authors.[221]

Jews understand why this list is deeply concerning. Because we've seen this playbook before. In 2022, the Boston Mapping Project[222] attempted to physically map Jewish organizations, businesses, and their affiliations, framing them as entities to be "disrupted" and "dismantled."[223] These weren't just abstract threats; they were tactics of intimidation, with actual addresses documented to incite fear and potential harm.

In the summer, on July 21st, 2024, Democratic Representative Ritchie Torres called out Chicago's City Lit Books for removing Korean-Jewish author Gabrielle Zevin's book *Tomorrow, and Tomorrow, and Tomorrow* from their book club for being "Zionist." Torres pointed out on his social media platform that since most Jews are Zionists, "the ban is tantamount to putting up a sign that reads: no Jews allowed."[224]

Then on October 28th, 2024, more than 1,000 authors and publishing insiders like Rachel Kushner, Sally Rooney, and Ta-Nehisi Coates pledged a "cultural boycott" of Jewish authors and Israeli publishers.[225]

Imagine banning books based on race. Why is antisemitism any different? Preventing our words will never erase our history. Our stories will in fact prevail.

THE BDS-DEI NEXUS: A DANGEROUS OVERLAP

Advocacy for Palestinian rights is framed through the lens of oppressors versus oppressed, casting Israel as the villain. This simplistic framing, championed by BDS and mirrored in many DEI programs, erases the Jewish community's historical and ongoing struggles with discrimination and violence.

The result is that Jewish students and professionals often feel alienated, excluded, and unsafe in spaces that champion "equity." The events following October 7th, when Hamas launched a horrific attack on Israeli civilians, exposed the biases within these frameworks. DEI offices at several universities remained silent about the atrocities against Israeli civilians but issued statements endorsing Palestinian "resistance," language drawn directly from BDS propaganda.

This normalization of extremism extended to platforms like TikTok, where Nashville-based DEI corporate consultant Noelle Johnson was playing dress-up promoting her "keffiyeh try-on sessions" mere weeks after the massacre, trivializing the tragedy and promoting symbols tied to jihadism and terrorism.

This is certainly not an attack on any Bedouin community or anyone in the Middle East wearing a headscarf of cultural significance. This is not about that. This is about women in the West specifically culturally appropriating the keffiyeh (many of whom couldn't even locate Gaza on a map prior to October 7th, or pronounce the name of the scarf itself).

She is neither Muslim nor Arab—and that matters. In the wake of women who were brutalized, their bodies shattered beyond repair, their pelvises crushed before they were executed simply for being part of the only democracy in the Middle East, Johnson, a DEI consultant, made a choice. Not to stand with the victims, not to condemn the terrorists, but to drape herself in the keffiyeh. A pattern that, in this context, was no symbol of peace, but an unmistakable show of allegiance to Hamas.

For an American woman to wear this scarf is not an act of solidarity; it is an embrace of Palestinian nationalism, a cause that Yasser Arafat wielded not for coexistence, but for destruction.[226] The keffiyeh became his uniform, his banner—not for a two-state solution, but for war. And under that banner, the Second Intifada was unleashed—a catastrophic bloodbath that left thousands dead. This is not a fashion statement in the United States. It is a signal. And we should pay attention.

BDS in Elementary School

Imagine if your child's elementary-school teacher appeared in a class wearing a swastika or a KKK hoodie. It would not happen. So why did the Metro Nashville public school system honor Bobbi Negrón, who proudly wore a keffiyeh while accepting her Teacher of the Year award? The keffiyeh is a violent symbol of terrorism that has zero place in our schools, especially worn by teachers.

Are educators reinforcing messages found on social media, or are they actively challenging the messages? Hopefully the latter. But judging from this, I don't know.

Tennessee adopted the International Holocaust Remembrance Alliance (IHRA) definition of antisemitism, and their willful ignorance of this issue is not just problematic. It demands immediate accountability.

BLM and DEI Connections

After October 7th, chapters of Black Lives Matter (BLM) openly expressed solidarity with Hamas, glorifying acts of terror under the guise of supporting Palestinian liberation. For example, BLM Chicago posted a graphic of a paraglider, a direct reference to the Hamas terrorists who paraglided into Israel to murder civilians.[227] DEI offices in institutions such as Harvard University and Columbia University failed to denounce the attacks, instead emphasizing one-sided narratives that mirrored BDS slogans.

Why October 7th Matters in the BDS-DEI Framework

The response to the events of October 7th revealed how DEI programs and organizations like BLM have become conduits for normalizing BDS rhetoric and justifying terror. These frameworks fail to account for Jewish experiences, creating environments where hatred is not only tolerated but actively encouraged under the guise of "equity and justice."

This overlap isn't accidental; it's a deliberate strategy by BDS and its affiliates to embed their anti-Israel agenda into the mainstream, capitalizing on social justice movements to obscure their ultimate goal: the delegitimization and destruction of Israel.

BDS as a Tax-Exempt Shelter for Terrorist Organizations

Behind its public image, BDS operates as a cover for funneling funds to terror groups. The tax-exempt status provides BDS groups legitimacy in the eyes of unsuspecting donors, shielding their deeper agenda from scrutiny.

Multiple investigations have revealed financial ties between BDS-affiliated organizations and Hamas, designated as a terrorist organization by the US and the EU.

US-based BDS groups exploit their 501(c)(3) status to raise money under the guise of "human rights," while channeling funds to groups like Islamic Jihad.

Former US Treasury Terror Financing Analyst, and current Foundation for Defense of Democracies Vice President Jonathan Schanzer testified on this very issue before Congress, saying, "AMP [American Muslims for Palestine] is arguably the most important sponsor and organizer for Students for Justice in Palestine, SJP, which is the most visible arm of the BDS campaign on campuses in the United States."[228]

Canary Mission further drives this home, exposing BDS as an alleged tax-exempt shelter for terrorism:

> In addition to providing financial public relations and legal assistance to SJP, AMP has also been accused of having connections to Hamas. The AMP National Board includes former members of both the Islamic Association of Palestine (IAP) and Holy Land Foundation (HLF), both of which were found liable for aiding and abetting Hamas.

Are we awake yet?

P.A.C.E.

A REFLECTIVE + INTERACTIVE DISCUSSION GUIDE FOR BOOK CLUBS

End BDS in Your Backyard

P PAUSE

Take a minute of silence to clear your mind and reflect on the chapter. During this pause, absorb your emotional responses without judgment, along with the impact of BDS on personal, societal, and political levels.

Guiding Questions for Reflection

1. What was your first thought or feeling when reading about BDS in this chapter? Reflect on how the movement is framed and its real-world impact on your screens or in your backyard.
2. Have you experienced or witnessed BDS in your community, college, or personal life? Consider how it affected free speech, inclusion, or Jewish students and professionals.

Silent Journal Reflection:

Write down your immediate reactions, emotions, and questions about BDS, along with its divisive nature and real consequences.

A ANALYZE

Think About BDS on State and Social Levels.

Group Activity: State-Level Analysis

- Research if your state has legislated against BDS, making it an anti-BDS state. Additionally, look into whether the state has codified the IHRA (International Holocaust Remembrance Alliance) definition of antisemitism.

- Look up bills related to BDS and ESG (Environmental, Social, Governance) ratings. ESG ratings can sometimes be used as a loophole for anti-Israel boycotts while maintaining a positive public image. Investigate local city and state politicians who have voted for or against such bills to understand political alignments and divisions.

Group Activity: Social-Level Analysis

- Create a list of universities in your state and research whether campus BDS organizations (like Students for Justice in Palestine or Jewish Voice for Peace) are active there.
- Research how these groups are influencing campus culture and political discourse. Consider what actions you might take to educate others or petition for awareness.

Questions for Group Discussion

- Do you understand the gravity of this subject? What other social movements have you seen BDS exploit?
- What global, political, or social forces are shaping the BDS movement, and how do these factors affect its efficacy?

Mind-Mapping Activity

Use a piece of paper or a digital whiteboard to visually expose the harm caused by BDS. Place "BDS" at the center, and add branches into key themes, ensuring each highlights its negative consequences.

- **Activism.** Misinformation and disinformation spreads through social media, creating hostility on campuses and silencing Jewish voices.

- **Politics.** BDS pressures governments and institutions to adopt anti-Israel policies, harming diplomatic relations and fueling antisemitic legislation.
- **Identity.** Jewish students and professionals face discrimination, exclusion from movements, and threats for supporting Israel.
- **Conflict**. BDS distorts history, ignores Palestinian leadership corruption, and promotes divisive rhetoric instead of solutions while also oppressing Palestinians.
- **Global Impact.** BDS disrupts industries, punishes companies working with Israel, and devastates Palestinian workers reliant on Israeli jobs.

As a group, discuss and draw connections between these branches. For example, consider how BDS campus activism (Activism) leads to institutional boycotts (Politics), which then embolden antisemitism (Identity) and economic harm (Global Impact). This exercise reveals that BDS is not a human rights effort, but a destructive Charlotte's Web force, exacerbating division and harming the very people it claims to help.

C CONTEMPLATE

Consider whether sanctions and boycotts truly help or worsen conflicts, particularly focusing on the unintended consequences.

Deep Dive into Case Studies

- Reflect on historical examples like the SodaStream boycott in 2005, where hundreds of Palestinians lost jobs due to the boycotts.
- Debate whether BDS-like actions in other countries (such as North Korea, Cuba, or Venezuela) have helped resolve conflicts, or deepened the suffering of the people they are meant to protect.

Discussion Questions

- How do sanctions and boycotts affect the people they are intended to help, particularly in the case of Palestinians in Gaza and Judea and Samaria?
- Does the BDS movement help or hurt Palestinians? What are the economic and social consequences of such distractions?

E ENGAGE

Take ACTION in your community, stay informed, and become vocal advocates for anti-BDS in your community on local, civic, collegiate, and corporate levels.

Brainstorming Action Plans

Engage participants in ways they can personally or collectively contribute to conversations about anti-BDS. What can they do to educate their community and reduce polarization on this topic? HBCUs, school boards, and local metro city councils are a great place to start.

Important Resources

1. AJC Campus BDS Backgrounder[229]
   https://www.ajc.org/campusbds.
2. Behind the Boycott: The History of the Hateful Campaign Against Israel[230]
   https://www.ajc.org/behindtheboycott.
3. Stand With Us Facts: What is BDS?[231]
   https://www.standwithus.com/factsheets-bds.
4. NGO Monitor[232]
   https://www.ngo-monitor.org/about/.

5. Honest Reporting: Jewish Voice for Peace[233]
   https://honestreporting.com/jewish-voice-for-peace-white washing-antisemitism-in-the-anti-israel-movement/.
6. ADL: BDS[234]
   https://forward.com/news/breaking-news/365434/adl-is-second-establishment-jewish-group-to-oppose-israel-s-anti-bds-law/.

Letter to Alyssa

I encourage you to write a direct message on social media or a letter to me reflecting on how this chapter has deepened or changed your understanding of advocacy, social justice, civic engagement, or political activism. I also encourage you to discuss in small groups how this book can be used as a tool to strengthen the safety within communities and create stronger bridges. I genuinely look forward to hearing from you.

CHAPTER 11

HUMAN NOT HEROIC

There are stories that often predate our earliest memories, inherited from those who cared for us, who loved us before we could even hold a single recollection of our own.

We all have them. From the fact that I was almost a ten-pound baby, sturdy, strong, stubborn, and full of promise, to how I was a decent sleeper and eater (obviously). These are the stories that often carry a certain tenderness: Joni Mitchell songs sung softly in the dark, first steps wobbly and proud, a favorite blanket clutched as if it were a steadfast companion, our first words, tiny victories, and shared belly laughter.

These are fragments of a past entrusted to us by others, pieced together from family anecdotes and blurry photographs. These moments, small and simple, are echoes of a time before our axons were fully myelinated. Yet somehow, we feel them deep in our bones.

But not every story is soft.

Not every memory handed down to us is wrapped in the comfort of safety.

Some stories are shadows that linger, even if we cannot fully recall them. They are the moments that shaped us before we could comprehend the weight of what was happening. They are whispered truths and sudden flashes of clarity, told to us in the hopes that we might someday understand the courage it takes to live in a world that is not always kind.

One of my earliest stories is not about playing dress-up or having imaginary friends. It unfolded at a swimming pool on a warm summer day in Tulsa, Oklahoma, in the 1980s.

Tulsa summers held their own kind of magic: hot concrete that warmed your toes, the cool relief of shimmering water, and my chunky toddler arms squeezed into floaties. In my swimsuit, with its pink ruffles fluttering as I splashed, I was unaware of anything beyond the pool's edge.

What started as a simple, sun-soaked afternoon at the Jewish Community Center swimming pool quickly turned into a mother's worst nightmare. The laughter and play of the pool faded into an echo as the warmth of the concrete gave way to the cold, tiled floor of a bathroom.

The weight of my mother's presence hovered over me, shielding me with her body. Her arms wrapped around me like they were immovable, her breath steady but strained, as if she was willing the world outside to stay at bay.

I was too young to understand the truth she was protecting me from: a sniper perched on a rooftop, threatening to shoot the women and children below. A summer day, so innocent, so young, turned to terror because of the simple fact of who we are. Jewish. Swimming, laughing, existing. And what we represent in the world.

At that moment, my mother wasn't trying to be heroic. She didn't act out of bravery, but out of instinct. Pure, human instinct. It wasn't about courage; it was about love. She shielded me not because she felt invincible, but because she didn't have a choice. This wasn't heroism. It was humanity—raw, unflinching grit, born from the primal need to protect her child so I could have the chance to live, to find my purpose, and to know my why.

This is where Judaism reveals itself—not as something grand or heroic, but as profoundly human.

It lives in the instinct to protect, in the unshakable bond of a mother shielding her child, and in the quiet choices we make to preserve life, fight for justice, and create peace. Judaism is not built on myths of perfection or unattainable ideals. It is grounded in the ordinary moments where love and responsibility intersect, where survival is elevated into something sacred.

The stories of our people are filled with this humanity. Of flawed individuals facing impossible choices, of enduring pain and carrying joy in the same breath. There is no room for hollow heroics in our history; instead, there is an understanding that to be Jewish is to hold the full weight of what it means to be alive. To be human.

It is the willingness to walk into uncertainty, to wrestle with questions, to acknowledge both the coexistence of the shadows and the light, and to choose a life of learning above all else. Because for all the terror and threats, there is also laughter at a swimming pool, the kind that bubbles up despite everything. There are candles lit in defiance of the shadows, their warm glow a quiet protest against the darkness. There are texts from my soldier friends in Gaza, their words carrying peace, presence, and prayer, a reminder of resilience in the midst of chaos. There are hands from the community, refusing to let anyone fall or go unseen. And there are fragments of stories—small and sacred—that weave through our lives, anchoring us to who we are and to the strength that carries us forward.

In this way, Judaism teaches us that humanity is heroism. Not in grand gestures, but in quiet corners, determined by daily acts of love and endurance.

In Western society, we exalt heroes, those who conquer, command attention, or defy impossible odds with extraordinary feats. We build monuments to them, write stories of their bravery into our collective memory, and strive to emulate their greatness. But in doing so, we often overlook the quiet humanity that sustains us: the instinct to protect, the commitment to care, and the courage to simply endure.

Our world increasingly values external success over internal virtue. We amplify spectacle over substance. The metrics of worth have shifted. From character to clout, from community to influence, from virtue to visibility. In this recalibration, the essence of humanity—our ability to connect, to nurture, and to build meaningful lives—has been quietly diminished, leaving us fractured in ways we are only beginning to understand.

Data paints a sobering picture: trust in institutions like family, faith, and even friendships is steadily declining. A Pew Research Center report found that 71 percent of Americans believe people are less confident in each other than they were two decades ago, and 64 percent say trust in the US federal government has eroded, complicating efforts to address societal challenges.[235] Civic engagement has waned, particularly among younger generations, with fewer participating in community organizations or voting. Empathy, too, has taken a hit; studies show younger generations exhibit lower levels of empathetic concern compared to their predecessors.[236]

Meanwhile, loneliness has reached epidemic proportions, with the US Surgeon General warning that social isolation poses health risks equivalent to smoking fifteen cigarettes a day. This epidemic contributes to increased risks of heart disease, stroke, dementia, depression, and anxiety.[237]

We are more connected than ever digitally, yet more isolated in spirit.

Judaism stands in quiet defiance of this erosion. Its values are not built on the spectacle of heroics but on the sacredness of everyday acts of love, humility, social responsibility, and community. It reminds us that human connection—rooted in kindness, in duty, in tradition—is what truly holds us together.

Take the moment with my mother at the pool: she wasn't performing for admiration or glory. She wasn't trying to be a hero. She was embodying something far more powerful: humanity. Her instinct to shield me came not from a place of grandeur, but from love. Judaism celebrates this very instinct, urging us to value the raw, unglamorous grit it takes to protect life, to preserve dignity, and to carry forward meaning despite everything.

In the face of a society that rewards the loudest, flashiest, or most "heroic," Judaism teaches us to value the quieter virtues: the resilience of a mother's embrace, the strength of community, the courage of vulnerability, and the willingness to enhance our lives. Not once, but again and again.

Our challenge today is to reclaim these values. To reject the transactional, the bursts for power, and the shallow, and to remember that our humanity, however imperfect, is what makes us whole.

Judaism doesn't ask us to be heroes; it asks us to be human. And in a world that increasingly forgets how, this might just be the most heroic act of all.

This quiet, steadfast humanity—the act of living with love and dignity, and challenging the many faces of hatred—is precisely what unleashed Hitler's crusade against the Jewish people. It wasn't just about annihilating a race; it was about attempting to erase a way of being that defies the world's obsession with power and spectacle. It's also what brought me to my most recent adventure in New York City.

DECEMBER 11TH, 2024

I arrived late the night before, my schedule crammed with back-to-back meetings. Tucked into the chaos was an invitation to a documentary screening about the roots of antisemitism.

It wasn't on my official itinerary, but I couldn't shake the pull to attend. I made time.

The stars aligned. With an unexpected gap in my day, I reached out to Alex, my partner in countless adventures. She was in town from Portugal, and we'd just been in Israel together that past February, walking streets heavy with history, healing, and resilience. Without hesitation, Alex agreed to join me.

As my driver navigated the stop-and-go traffic toward the Park East Synagogue, the sound of the windshield wipers created a steady rhythm against the backdrop of New York's restless energy. The hum of the city surrounded me, its urgency palpable, but inside the car, I felt an unusual stillness. I wasn't just heading to a film. I was heading into an exploration of one of humanity's most persistent hatreds: antisemitism.

The screening, hosted by author and filmmaker Rabbi Raphael Shore, who had flown in from Israel, offered a perspective on the roots of antisemitism that has been glaringly overlooked by both academia and history. This was not simply another recounting of a past genocide or a detailed inventory of prejudice. It was a deeply thought-provoking exploration of why antisemitism is so uniquely persistent, universal, and devastatingly adaptable. The film sought to illuminate forces that have not waned but have instead evolved, embedding themselves into societies across centuries and now permeating the digital landscapes of our own living rooms.

Rabbi Shore's lens is one of humility and truth as he confronted conventional narratives, raising unsettling and often ignored questions. How could Germany, arguably one of the most educated, progressive, and culturally sophisticated nations of its time, descend into such unspeakable barbarism? What common ground did Hitler share with rabbis of his time? Yes, you read that correctly. Why did Hitler truly seek to annihilate the Jews? (Hint: it wasn't because of our faults, but because of our virtues.) How did antisemitism spread and intensify in the Arab world, becoming a pervasive ideology? And perhaps most disturbingly, why do these patterns remain not only relevant but so potent in today's fractured, polarized world?

This was no ordinary documentary.

It wasn't just a retelling of history. It was a mirror , held up to history, to the Jews, to Israel, and to anything that threatens to dismantle authoritative regimes. The reflection it cast was not merely of past horrors but of the very real dangers still alive in the present.

It forced those of us gathered on that rainy Manhattan night to confront undeniable truths. Truths that connected visible patterns of hatred and violence, which continue to persist with alarming ease. These patterns, once buried beneath the veil of history, were now laid bare before us, demanding our attention.

As the Park East Synagogue came into view and the city lights blurred through the rain, I tightened my grip on my umbrella. The weight of these revelations settled within me. Not as despair, but as an important call to action. This film wasn't just about remembering the past; it was about arming ourselves to confront the very real echoes of that history in our own time. With every step closer to the synagogue, I felt the responsibility grow heavier, more resolute. I knew I was not just attending a screening; I was stepping into a conversation that had to be heard, understood, and carried forward.

The stories and lessons shared that night would not, and could not, be ignored.

I sat in the front row of the synagogue, next to my friends Alex and Lizzie, and settled in to view the documentary, and I heard the words: Hitler wasn't a madman.

Huh?

I leaned in, to listen to experts and historians break down this concept.

> In order to properly understand this we must consider the Nazi worldview. Hitler believed that there was one great conflict that drives human history, and that was the idea of survival of the fittest. Hitler believed that if Jewish ideas of humanitarianism, love, equality, democracy were to succeed, that would be the end of humanity.—Rabbi Shore

I turned over the words in my mind. Survival of the fittest? Natural selection?

It's like Jews were Katniss up against President Snow in the Hunger Games.

Shore explained that up until World War II, the Jews living in Germany's Weimar Republic were well assimilated, even known for eating pork and having Christmas trees.

Marked by the establishment of a democratic government in the aftermath of World War I, the Weimar Republic, from 1919 to 1933, was a transformative era in Germany. This period not only ushered in art, music, philosophy, and literature, but also embodied a profoundly progressive movement aimed at expanding LGBTQ+ rights, addressing economic challenges caused by hyperinflation, promoting gender equality, and fostering collective action.

However, it also became fertile ground for extremist ideologies, including the rise of the Nazi Party.[238]

In the wake of the Great Depression, the Nazis exploited widespread despair, scapegoating Jews and promising stability to a disillusioned public. This period reveals just how fragile democracy is, especially when a nation lacks a strong social identity and has deep divisions between liberal and conservative political parties. The Nazis strategically positioned themselves as a disciplined, authoritarian alternative to the perceived chaos, offering a sense of order and belonging.

Strikingly similar to the present day Pro-Palestinian cause, the rhetoric of social justice and human rights was co-opted and manipulated during this time, becoming a pathway for Hitler's rise to power. (Does this sound familiar?)

My thoughts are loud. History is repeating itself, and I find myself living in a country where too few seem to remember it. The weight of ignorance is suffocating me in the synagogue.

> Rabbi Shore's documentary drives the point home: They were the most assimilated Jews ever, and that was the epicenter of the same movement . . . Hitler never viewed the Jews as a physical threat. We were a spiritual and moral threat . . . The Rabbis of the Talmud and Adolf Hitler actually agree on the root cause of antisemitism, that the root of antisemitism was actually Sinai.[239]

The Torah tells the story of Moses receiving the Ten Commandments on top of Mount Sinai from G-d, who entrusted the Israelites to bring morality, ethics, and monotheism into the world.

Hermann Rauschning, who briefly joined the Nazi party before renouncing it, said: "It's got to get out of our blood, the curse from Mount Sinai. The day will come when I shall hold up against those commandments, the tablets of a new law."

Watching the documentary in the dimly lit synagogue in Manhattan, a light bulb went off in my mind. I had never encountered this framing of the Holocaust before: Hitler didn't want to annihilate the Jews because he saw us as vermin, rats, or subhuman. He wanted to eradicate us because of the moral and spiritual light we carry. A light rooted in the ethics and morals originating from the Ten Commandments on Mount Sinai. This light challenges all authoritarian regimes, including his own.

G-d calls the Israelites to be light-bearers, bringing the gifts of knowledge, freedom, and equality to the world. Hitler sought to extinguish that light, ensuring it would never spread.

The last half of Shore's documentary explored the relationship between Nazis and Islamists.

My jaw nearly hit the floor. It's almost heartwarming, in a deeply twisted way, to see two psychopaths finding common ground.

In 1941, Haj Amin al-Husseini, the Grand Mufti of Jerusalem and a key figure in the Palestinian nationalist movement and religious leader in the Muslim world, was expelled from the Middle East and was granted asylum and lavish digs in Nazi-occupied Berlin. There, he collaborated with Adolf Hitler, and the two forged an alliance based on their mutual hatred of Jews. In their meeting, Hitler promised al-Husseini that, after completing his genocide in Europe, he would turn his attention to the Holy Land to finish the extermination of the Jewish people. This dark moment in history underscores the sinister bond between Nazi ideology and Palestinian indoctrination.[240]

From Berlin, Haj Amin al-Husseini used Axis radio broadcasts, interpreted in more than twelve languages, to spread dangerous anti-Allied and antisemitic propaganda, as documented by the *Holocaust Encyclopedia*.[241] He promoted the idea of a "global Jewish conspiracy," claiming that Jews were "controlling the US and British governments," while framing them as enemies of Islam and comparing them to a dangerous disease. Al-Husseini's broadcasts not only incited violence but also called for insurrections, urging Arabs to kill Jews wherever they encountered them and demanding their expulsion from Arab lands. In 1943, he met with SS chief Heinrich Himmler, deepening his collaboration with the Nazi regime and rallying Arab and Muslim communities to support the Axis powers.

As the Germans surrendered and World War II neared its end, al-Husseini returned to Cairo, where he continued to spread anti-Zionist and antisemitic rhetoric. He soon became closely aligned with Hassan al-Banna, the leader of the Muslim Brotherhood. In 1946, al-Banna declared, "Germany and Hitler are gone, but Amin al-Husseini will continue the struggle. The Mufti is Palestine, and Palestine is the Mufti." This statement underscores the dangerous legacy of the Mufti, whose influence only deepened the radicalization of the Brotherhood, a movement that would later give rise to Hamas, a globally recognized terrorist organization.

Al-Husseini's poisonous ideology in eradicating the Jewish State also had a lasting impact on his relative, Yasser Arafat, who adopted the Mufti's vision of violent Palestinian nationalism. Al-Husseini's legacy continues to be honored by figures like Palestinian Authority President Mahmoud Abbas, who praises him as a "hero."

This is a tangled web of totalitarian ideologies stretching across generations. Jihadism has picked up where Nazi Germany left off, continuing the mission to exterminate Jews, now masked in a new guise. The genocidal hatred that fueled the Holocaust is not gone. It lives on, repackaged.

This is not about land.

This is not about freedom.

This is about darkness.

Islamists are the new Nazis.

The Holocaust will not be over until Hitler's ideology is buried in the Arab world.

> The mission of the Jewish people has never been to make the world more Jewish, but to make it more human.
>
> Elie Wiesel

This is our light.

History's evils do not linger because they are forgotten; they remain because we fail to see their shape in the present. The forces that seek to erase our values, morality, ethics, and meaning do not vanish with time. They adapt. They camouflage. They wait for the world to look away.

But being human means we do not look away.

To be human is to remember. Not passively, not as a relic of the past, but as a responsibility to the future. It is to recognize that hatred, unchecked, does not stay in one place. That silence is its accomplice. That indifference, dressed as neutrality, is a choice with severe consequences.

Each of us, in our own way, stands at a threshold between memory and action. And the question is not whether history will repeat. It is whether we will allow it to.

In a world obsessed with power, we can persist with purpose. In an era of division, we can insist on connection. And in a culture that rewards rage, we can return, again and again, to the quiet, steady work of being fully, fiercely, bravely alive.

What endures are the small, defiant acts of humanity. A parent showing up at a school board meeting to stand for what's right. A family setting aside technology to share a meal and truly listen to one another. Neighbors checking in just to say, "I see you, I'm here." It's the friend who holds your hand through a mammogram, the choice to pause before jumping to conclusions online, the commitment to remain respectful and connected even after deep disagreements.

It is the leader who, even in a darkened world, opens a book and teaches history, knowing that learning is an act of survival. It is the steadfast belief that to save and heal one life is to save the world. The insistence that justice and kindness are not opposing forces but intertwined obligations. The refusal to let suffering harden the heart, to let fear define the future, to let darkness be met with anything but light.

Because these are not grand gestures. They are the quiet, everyday moments where goodness is a choice. These are the choices that define us.

To resist hatred. To choose kindness. To love with an open heart. These are not acts of heroism, but responsibilities. And that responsibility, that light—it belongs to us all.

These are not heroic acts.

They are human ones.

Because in the end, it's not heroism that saves us.

It's our humanity.

Being a hero is simply being human.

P.A.C.E.

A REFLECTIVE + INTERACTIVE DISCUSSION GUIDE FOR BOOK CLUBS

Be a Human

As we near the end of this journey, I invite you and your book club to reflect on a deeply meaningful exercise, one that extends beyond the pages of this book and into real life. This activity focuses on relationships that were lost or strained due to political divides or geopolitical tensions. Often these divisions can create lasting rifts, not only in families but within communities.

We will work to bring awareness to those moments of disconnection and explore pathways to healing. It is an invitation to take responsibility for moving forward, whether by seeking reconciliation or simply releasing the weight of unresolved tension.

The goal is to focus on finding the center within the conversation rather than changing someone's worldview.

P PAUSE

Take a moment to reflect on any relationships within your personal circle that were affected or damaged by political or ideological disagreements from either side of the political aisle. These could be friends, family, or colleagues. Let yourself feel the weight of that loss and acknowledge how it affected you.

Prompts

- Think of a person or relationship that changed due to political differences or a foreign conflict. What was the turning point? How did it feel when the rift began to form?
- How has this divide affected you personally? Consider how it has affected them.

A ANALYZE

Consider the reasons behind the disconnect. What were the fundamental disagreements or misunderstandings? Reflect on the issue: the emotions, beliefs, or actions that fueled the divide. Were these differences resolvable with education or facts, or did they reflect a deeper cultural, ideological, or personal rift?

Prompts

- What were the primary causes of the split? Was it a particular issue that felt too divisive to move past? Were there moments where the conversation could have taken a different turn?
- How might you now see both perspectives with greater empathy?

C CONTEMPLATE

Reflect on the importance of the relationship itself. Consider whether there is space for a new kind of connection—one built not on agreement, but on respect and mutual understanding. The goal is not to change the other person's views but to meet them in a place of shared humanity, where differences can exist without eroding the relationship.

Prompts

- What would it look like to reconnect with this person from a place of respect, even without agreeing on the political issue?
- How can you find common ground in your shared humanity, rather than focusing on your differences?
- What steps would be necessary to move forward with compassion?
- What did you know—or not know—about Yasser Arafat's connection to Nazi-aligned leaders like Amin al-Husseini? How does this history challenge mainstream narratives about the Israel-Palestine conflict?

- What do you make of the shared genetic heritage between Jewish and Arab populations? How does this complicate the "colonizer" narrative?
- How can understanding historical alliances and ideological cross-pollination help us recognize manipulation in today's discourse?

E ENGAGE

The final step is to take meaningful action. This could mean reaching out with an open mind, offering a gesture of goodwill, or simply engaging in a conversation where both sides are heard without the pressure to agree. The focus is on restoring connection, rather than debating or convincing, by fostering a dialogue grounded in empathy.

Prompts

- What small step can you take this week to open the door for dialogue?
- Could you send a message, ask to reconnect, or have a simple conversation focused on understanding each other rather than persuading one another?

Allow this process to be about repair, not about changing minds, by reconnecting through shared experiences, our humanness, and mutual respect.

ACKNOWLEDGMENTS

This book was born from rupture—and from fierce, unrelenting hope. It was shaped in the aftermath of loss. It was written in defiance of silence.

To write is to risk. To tell the truth is to lose things. I lost a book deal. Because I am Jewish. Because I refused to shrink. I refused to play the game. I refused to trade creativity for comfort. And still, I wrote.

Because I hate bullies. Because I loathe injustice—especially the kind that hides behind silence.

This book is a bridge—between lives stolen too soon and the stories that still long to be reclaimed. It is built from loss and love, from rage and reverence, from endings that birthed beginnings.

To those who quietly stepped away—or loudly left—thank you.

You were part of the journey. Your absence made room for my becoming.

Growth requires goodbye. I hold no bitterness—only clarity.

To those who stayed—you are the heartbeat of these pages.

You sat with me in the fire, in the grief, in the sacred mess of discomfort.

You held space for the tears, the laughter, the anger, and the truth.

You never looked away. This is your love letter.

To my literary agent, Ami McConnell—you believed in me in a way I hadn't yet believed in myself. You protected my light. You fought for this book. You refused to accept "no" on my behalf. Your loyalty is rare. Your friendship is sacred. Thank you for helping me bring this vision to life.

To Lena Abraham, who became family—I'll never forget our first Zoom: a Syrian Christian who survived the Arab Spring, and a White Blonde Jew . . . it sounds like the start of a joke. But what followed was no joke—it was trust, alignment, and fire. Your encouragement and weekly calls are what pushed this project across the finish line in just five months. You reminded me that I am a writer. You believed this work could ripple outward and create change. You reminded me that healing is advocacy, advocacy is action, and action is love. Thank you—for your faith, your friendship, and your fight.

To my sisterhood—you know who you are. Writers. Dreamers. Truth-tellers. Community-builders. Mentors. Challengers. Accountability partners. We are women who hold fire in one hand and love in the other.

To my mother and my sister—thank you for showing me what resilience looks like in motion. You are both stitched into my strength, even when the threads felt invisible.

To the women who chose me—and stayed—you are my chosen family. Your love is unconditional, your presence unwavering, your wisdom fierce. I am endlessly grateful for the ways you've held me, pushed me, protected me, and reminded me of who I am—especially when I forgot. I can't wait to see where we all go next. May the path be new, brave, and paved with prosperity and peace.

To every delegation that brought me to Israel—from the American Jewish Committee to Christians United for Israel—thank you for granting me the access to bear witness. It was in these rooms, and through the connections that followed—with professors, policymakers, journalists, warriors, hostages, Nova Music Festival survivors, hostage family members, ambassadors, and diplomats—that I began to understand the full weight of this moment in history. Because of you, I found the strength to stand taller. To speak louder. To become a resource for a region of the United States where access to these truths is rare—and desperately needed.

And to the voices taken too soon—you are woven into every word of this book. I will never stop speaking your names. This work is for you. To bear witness is not just an act of remembrance—it is a responsibility. May your stories awaken courage. May your memory ignite curiosity. And may your legacy remind the world: we must never look away.

To the team at BenBella Books, and to my editor, Rick—thank you for your courage and care. You heard my voice when others were too afraid to listen. You took a risk. You honored the integrity of this work. I will never forget that.

To Nate Griffin—you've said yes to every wild idea and unexpected pivot. You've been with me since the beginning, and I've always felt safe in front of your lens. This is the second cover we've created together, and I treasure your eye, your heart, and your friendship. Thank you for walking beside me.

To those I cannot name—at least not yet—thank you.

You came in war. One as an ending. One as a fire. One as peace.

You each held a mirror to something I needed to see.

One reminded me of what I had to let go of. One awakened a part of me I thought had died. One showed me that safety doesn't have to be earned through survival. You fought on different planes—in silence, on battlefields, with intellect. You taught me about loyalty, desire, and stillness. You taught me about absence. And presence. Through all of it—every ache, every awakening—I found something unthinkable: Peace. Love. Myself. I hope, wherever you are, in whatever war you now face—you find yours too.

This book is a prayer, a protest, and a promise.

To anyone who's ever been silenced: keep speaking.

To anyone who's ever been exiled for telling the truth: come closer.

We are not meant to walk through fire alone.

This book is proof that healing is a shared act.

It is also a reminder that truth-telling may cost you comfort—but it will give you back your soul.

Let this be your permission slip.

To speak louder. To stand taller. To begin again.

NOTES

1. Daniel Byman et al., "Hamas's October 7 Attack: Visualizing the Data," Commentary, Center for Strategic and International Studies, December 19, 2023, https://www.csis.org/analysis/hamass-october-7-attack-visualizing-data.
2. Lucy Williamson, "Israel Gaza: Hamas Raped and Mutilated Women on 7 October, BBC Hears," BBC News, December 5, 2023, https://www.bbc.com/news/world-middle-east-67629181.
3. Isabel Kershner, "A Legacy of Sexual Violence: Hamas's October 7 Attacks on Israel," *The New York Times*, December 28, 2023, https://www.nytimes.com/2023/12/28/world/middleeast/oct-7-attacks-hamas-israel-sexual-violence.html.
4. "Israel-Gaza Hamas War: Palestinians Photo Gallery," AP News, October 2023, https://apnews.com/article/israel-gaza-hamas-war-palcstinians photo-gallery-0d3960dc03ddd8b4fe3d81111cf177a0.
5. "POY 81 Impact 2023: Israel-Hamas War Picture Story," The Reynolds Journalism Institute, https://poy.org/81/13.html.
6. Alison Leigh Cowan, "And the Prize for Photography Goes to . . . Hamas?" *Tablet*, May 1, 2024, https://www.tabletmag.com/sections/arts-letters/articles/prize-for-photography-goes-to-hamas.
7. "Photographers Without Borders: AP, Reuters Pictures of Hamas Atrocities Raise Ethical Questions," HonestReporting, November 8, 2023. https://honestreporting.com/photographers-without-borders-ap-reuters-pictures-of-hamas-atrocities-raise-ethical-questions/.

8. "The State of Antisemitism in America 2025," American Jewish Committee, accessed February 15, 2026, https://www.ajc.org/AntisemitismReport2025/InsightsandAnalysis.
9. Christopher Paul, "Germany and Japan: Reconciliation and Responsibility," Johns Hopkins University Hub, Summer 2015, https://hub.jhu.edu/magazine/2015/summer/germany-japan-reconciliation/.
10. Justice in Post-Nazi Western Germany." Accessed March 16, 2025. https://www.nationalww2museum.org/war/articles/justice-in-post-nazi-western-germany.
11. David Pollock and Catherine Cleveland, "What Do Palestinians Want?" The Washington Institute for Near East Policy, July 23, 2021, https://www.washingtoninstitute.org/policy-analysis/what-do-palestinians-want.
12. Gadi Taub, "Sorry, but There Is No Two-State Solution," *Tablet*, February 12, 2024, https://www.tabletmag.com/sections/israel-middle-east/articles/sorry-there-is-no-two-state-solution.
13. Ali Rashid Al Nuaimi, "Four Pillars of Moral Education in UAE," Alira Shi Dal Nuai Ali Rashid Al Nuaimi, accessed March 20, 2025, https://www.alirashidalnuaimi.com/four-pillars-of-moral-education-in-uae/.
14. The Foundation for Defense of Democracies, accessed May 27, 2025, https://www.fdd.org.
15. Douglas Murray, *The War on the West* (Broadside Books, 2022).
16. Ayaan Hirsi Ali, *Heretic: Why Islam Needs a Reformation Now* (Harper, 2015).
17. Martin Luther King Jr., "I Have a Dream," delivered August 28, 1963, at the Lincoln Memorial, Washington, DC.
18. Civil Rights Act of 1964, Pub. L. No. 88-352, 78 Stat. 241 (1964).
19. CM-607 Affirmative Action," US Equal Employment Opportunity Commission, accessed March 16, 2025, https://www.eeoc.gov/laws/guidance/cm-607-affirmative-action.
20. "DEI Origins: How Diversity, Equity, and Inclusion Evolved," This Is DEI, September 22, 2021, https://www.thisisdei.com/blog/dei-origins-how-diversity-equity-and-inclusion-evolved.

21. "Glossary of Definitions and Core Concepts for Diversity, Equity, and Inclusion (DEI)," AcademyHealth, November 9, 2021, https://academyhealth.org/sites/default/files/publication/%5Bfield_date%3Acustom%3AY%5D-%5Bfield_date%3Acustom%3Am%5D/dei glossary_nov_2021_1.pdf.
22. "We Need to Say Goodbye to DEI," The Tufts Daily, March 2915, 2024. https://www.tuftsdaily.com/article/2024/03/we-need-to-say-goodbye-to-dei.
23. Nicquel Terry Ellis, "What Is DEI, and Why Is It Dividing America?" CNN, January 22, 2025, https://www.cnn.com/2025/01/22/us/dei-diversity-equity-inclusion-explained.
24. Zev Stub, "FBI Says Anti-Jewish Hate Crimes across US Hit Record High in 2024," *The Times of Israel*, August 5, 2025, https://www.timesofisrael.com/fbi-says-anti-jewish-hate-crimes-across-us-hit-record-high-in-2024/.
25. Anti-Defamation League, "Anti-Jewish Hate Crimes Comprised Nearly 70% of All Religion-Based Hate Crimes in 2024, FBI Reports," press release, August 5, 2025, https://www.adl.org/resources/press-release/anti-jewish-hate-crimes-comprised-nearly-70-all-religion-based-hate-crimes.
26. Armin Rosen, "The DEI Complex Will Never Protect Jews," *Tablet*, October 25, 2023, https://www.tabletmag.com/sections/news/articles/the-dei-complex-will-never-protect-jews.
27. "Instructing Animosity: The Use of Online Spaces to Incite Violence and Hatred How DEI Pedagogy Produces the Hostile Attribution Bias," Network Contagion Research Institute, November 13, 2024, https://networkcontagion.us/wp-content/uploads/Instructing-Animosity_11.13.24.pdf.
28. Jonathan Harounoff, "How DEI Is Failing Jewish Workers in the Era of Facing Rising Antisemitism," *New York Post*, February 3, 2024, https://nypost.com/2024/02/03/news/dei-is-failing-jewish-workers-facing-rising-antisemitism/.
29. "Zev Stub, "Survey: A Third of US Jews Have Experienced Antisemitism, 3/4 Feel Less Safe," *The Times of Israel*, February 12, 2025,

https://www.timesofisrael.com/survey-a-third-of-us-jews-have-experienced-antisemitism-3-4-feel-less-safe/.

30. Jay Greene and James Paul, "The Inclusion Delusion: The Antisemitism of Diversity, Equity, and Inclusion Staff at Universities," The Heritage Foundation, December 8, 2021, https://www.heritage.org/education/report/inclusion-delusion-the-antisemitism-diversity-equity-and-inclusion-staff.
31. "1 in 4 Hiring Managers Say They Are Less Likely to Move Forward with Jewish Applicants," Resume Builder, November 21, 2022, https://www.resumebuilder.com/1-in-4-hiring-managers-say-they-are-less-likely-to-move-forward-with-jewish-applicants/.
32. "American Jews and Israeli Americans Experience Substantial Discrimination," Anti-Defamation League, accessed December 1, 2024, https://www.adl.org/resources/press-release/american-jews-and-israeli-americans-experience-substantial-discrimination.
33. Coleman Hughes, *The End of Race Politics: Arguments for a Colorblind Society* (Threshold Editions, 2024).
34. Corey Brooks, "America Works. DEI Doesn't," *Tablet*, January 16, 2024, https://www.tabletmag.com/sections/news/articles/america-works-dei-doesnt.
35. John Sailer, "How DEI Is Supplanting Truth as the Mission of American Universities," *The Free Press*, January 9, 2023, https://www.thefp.com/p/how-dei-is-supplanting-truth-as-the.
36. David L. Bernstein, *Woke Antisemitism: How a Progressive Ideology Harms Jews* (Wicked Son, 2022).
37. Thomas Sowell, *Social Justice Fallacies* (Basic Books, 2023).
38. https://www.census.gov/library/stories/2021/08/improved-race-ethnicity-measures-reveal-united-states-population-much-more-multiracial.html#:~:text=Coupled%20with%20the,population)%20in%202020.
39. Roland G. Fryer Jr., "An Empirical Analysis of Racial Differences in Police Use of Force," National Bureau of Economic Research, July 2016, https://www.nber.org/papers/w22399.

40. "Neturei Karta," Anti-Defamation League, accessed March 17, 2025, https://www.adl.org/resources/backgrounder/neturei-karta.
41. Jonathan Saul, "Anti-Israel 'Rabbis' Face Fallout from Jewish World," Reuters, last modified October 21, 2023, https://www.reuters.com/article/world/anti-israel-rabbis-face-fallout-from-jewish-world-idUSL21860038.
42. March 3 Instagram Post, @ihartericka, Instagram, March 3, 2025.
43. "Working Definition of Antisemitism," International Holocaust Remembrance Alliance, accessed March 17, 2025. https://holocaustremembrance.com/resources/working-definition-antisemitism#:~:text=%E2%80%9CAntisemitism%20is%20a%20certain%20perception,community%20institutions%20and%20religious%20facilities.%E2%80%9D.
44. "Zionist/'Zio,'" American Jewish Committee, accessed March 17, 2025, https://www.ajc.org/translatehate/Zionist.
45. "Jewish Americans in 2020," Pew Research Center, May 11, 2021, https://www.pewresearch.org/wp-content/uploads/sites/20/2021/05/PF_05.11.21_Jewish.Americans.pdf.
46. "What Is Anti-Zionism?" American Jewish Committee, accessed March 17, 2025, https://www.ajc.org/news/anti-zionism-and-antisemitism.
47. The Editors of Encyclopaedia Britannica, "Nation of Islam," *Encyclopaedia Britannica*, accessed March 17, 2025, https://www.britannica.com/topic/Nation-of-Islam.
48. Dana W. White, "Why HBCUs Are Key to Fighting Antisemitism," Sapir, November 18, 2024, https://sapirjournal.org/university/2024/11/why-hbcus-are-key-to-fighting-antisemitism/.
49. "Farrakhan Responds to Israel-Hamas War with Antisemitic Conspiracy Theories at Saviours' Day," Anti-Defamation League, February 27, 2024, https://www.adl.org/resources/article/farrakhan-responds-israel-hamas-war-antisemitic-conspiracy-theories-saviours-day#:~:text=Farrakhan's%20speech%20reflected%20the%20NOI's,antisemitic%2C%20conspiratorial%20claims%20about%20Israel.

50. Coleman Hughes, "The History and Ethics of the Israel-Palestine Conflict with Dr. Benny Morris," *Conversations with Coleman* (podcast), The Free Press, September 1, 2023.
51. Dana W. White, "Why HBCUs Are Key to Fighting Antisemitism," Sapir, November 18, 2024, https://sapirjournal.org/university/2024/11/why-hbcus-are-key-to-fighting-antisemitism/.
52. Anti-Defamation League. "Farrakhan Responds to Israel-Hamas War with Antisemitic Conspiracy Theories at Saviours' Day," https://www.adl.org/resources/article/farrakhan-responds-israel-hamas-war-antisemitic-conspiracy-theories-saviours-day#:~:text=Farrakhan's%20speech%20reflected%20the%20NOI's,antisemitic%2C%20conspiratorial%20claims%20about%20Israel.
53. "Farrakhan: In His Own Words," Anti-Defamation League, accessed March 17, 2025, https://www.adl.org/resources/backgrounder/farrakhan-his-own-words#:~:text=Farrakhan%20has%20alleged%20that%20the,the%20media%20and%20Hollywood%2C%20as.
54. Pew Research Center. "Key Findings About Black Immigrants in the U.S." January 27, 2022, https://www.pewresearch.org/short-reads/2022/01/27/key-findings-about-black-immigrants-in-the-u-s/.
55. Gil Troy, *Tablet*, "How Palestine Hijacked the U.S. Civil Rights Movement," accessed December 1, 2024, https://www.tabletmag.com/sections/news/articles/how,palestine,hijacked,us,civil,rights,movement/.
56. Bari Weiss, *How to Fight Anti-Semitism* (Crown Publishing, 2019).
57. Douglas Murray, *The Madness of Crowds: Gender, Race and Identity* (Bloomsbury Continuum, 2019).
58. David Baddiel, *Jews Don't Count* (The Times Literary Supplement, 2021).
59. Benny Morris, *1948: A History of the First Arab-Israeli War* (Yale University Press, 2009).
60. Sam Harris, "Why Don't I Criticize Israel?" *Making Sense* (podcast), July 27, 2014, https://www.samharris.org/podcasts/making-sense-episodes/why-dont-i-criticize-israel.
61. Marc Schneier, *Shared Dreams: Martin Luther King Jr. and the Jewish Community* (Jewish Lights Publishing, 1999).

62. Mathilda Heller, "Jewish Schoolgirls Attacked by Man Hurling Glass Bottles in London, One Badly Wounded," *The Jerusalem Post*, November 26, 2024, https://www.jpost.com/diaspora/article-830827.
63. Jackson Walker, "Democrat Condemns Steam for October 7 Massacre Video Game: 'Barbaric,'" CBS Austin, December 26, 2024, https://cbsaustin.com/news/nation-world/ritchie-torres-condemns-steam-for-october-7-massacre-video-game-barbaric-rep-ritchie-torres-democrat-ny-friday-condemned-video-game-giant-steam-for-allowing-sales-of-a-game-which-lets-players-control-a-palestinian-terrorist-as-they-slay-jewish-israelis.
64. "American Jews and Israeli Americans Experience Substantial Discrimination in the U.S. Job Market, ADL Study Finds," Anti-Defamation League, December 4, 2024, https://www.adl.org/resources/press-release/american-jews-and-israeli-americans-experience-substantial-discrimination.
65. Benita Kolovos, "Melbourne Synagogue Fire a Terrorist Attack 'on the Jewish People,' Police Believe," *The Guardian*, December 8, 2024, https://www.theguardian.com/australia-news/2024/dec/09/melbourne-adass-israel-synagogue-fire-ripponlea-suspected-terrorist-attack-ntwnfb#:~:text=Victoria%20police%20say%20Friday's%20arson,terrorist%20attack%20on%20Monday%20morning.
66. "2 Kindergarteners Wounded and Gunman Dead After Shooting at California Religious School," AP News, updated December 5, 2024, https://apnews.com/article/butte-county-california-school-shooting-843b6fe4ed0e13b863f696e630dbf0a6.
67. Michael Starr, "UCLA Student Culture Group Accused of Hiring Discrimination Against Jews," *The Jerusalem Post*, December 4, 2024, https://www.jpost.com/diaspora/antisemitism/article-831990.
68. Morgan Fogarty, "Local Woman's Home Spray-Painted with Swastikas and Anti-Gay Slurs," WCCB Charlotte, December 9, 2024, https://www.wccbcharlotte.com/2024/12/09/local-womans-home-spray-painted-with-swastikas-and-anti-gay-slurs/.
69. Sharon Weinberg, "Antisemitic Graffiti Found at East Greenwich, RI, High School in RI," *The Boston Globe*, December 6, 2024,

https://www.bostonglobe.com/2024/12/06/metro/antisemitic-graffiti-east-greenwich-high-school-ri/.

70. Isabel Keane, "Israeli Locksmith Murdered in Memphis After Being Lured out on a Job," *New York Post*, November 24, 2024, https://nypost.com/2024/11/24/us-news/murder-of-israeli-locksmith-in-tenn-raises-terrorism-fears-report/.
71. "Pro-Palestinians Celebrate Hamas Attack as Israel Supporters Rally in New York," *The Times of Israel*, November 2024, https://www.timesofisrael.com/pro-palestinians-celebrate-hamas-attack-as-israel-supporters-rally-in-new-york/.
72. Angela Fortuna, "Greenwich Elementary School-Aged Kid Hits Another Child Due to Her Religion: Police," NBC Connecticut, November 19, 2024, https://www.nbcconnecticut.com/news/local/greenwich-elementary-school-aged-kid-hits-another-child-religion/3437120/.
73. "Swastika Sent to Jewish Students, Labelled Non-Hate Crime by UK Police," *The Jerusalem Post*, November 18, 2024, https://www.jpost.com/diaspora/antisemitism/article-829566.
74. Ron Zeitlinger, "Hoboken Stirs Controversy with Palestinian 'Flag Raising' Event at City Hall," *The Jersey Journal*, November 25, 2024, https://www.nj.com/hudson/2024/11/hoboken-stirs-controversy-with-palestinian-flag-raising-event-at-city-hall.html.
75. "Rabbi Zvi Kogan, 28, Murdered by Terrorists," Chabad.org, November 24, 2024, https://www.chabad.org/news/article_cdo/aid/6675476/jewish/Rabbi-Zvi-Kogan-28-Murdered-by-Terrorists.htm.
76. Mathilda Heller, "Over 50,000 Quebec Students Join Riots Where Calls for Intifada, Final Solution Are Voiced," *The Jerusalem Post*, November 22, 2024, https://www.jpost.com/diaspora/article-83027#google_vignette.
77. Michael E. Dyson, "Blacks and Jews, Again," *The New York Times*, November 20, 2022, ""https://www.nytimes.com/2022/11/20/opinion/kyrie-irving-kanye-west-antisemitism.html.
78. F. James Davis, *Who Is Black? One Nation's Definition* (Pennsylvania State University Press, 1991).

79. "One Drop Rule Defined," PBS Frontline, accessed December 1, 2024, https://www.pbs.org/wgbh/pages/frontline/shows/jefferson/mixed/onedrop.html.
80. The Editors of Encyclopaedia Britannica, "Levant," Encyclopaedia Britannica, last updated July 22, 2025, https://www.britannica.com/place/Levant.
81. Daniel 7:2,7 (The Tanakh: The Holy Scriptures, The New JPS Translation, Jewish Publication Society, 1999).
82. Historical dates from Mattis Kantor, Codex Judaica (Zichron Press, March 2006).
83. Rabbi Dovie Schochet, "Discover the Four Exiles of the Jewish People," Chabad.org, accessed March 17, 2025, https://www.chabad.org/library/article_cdo/aid/3671017/jewish/Discover-the-Four-Exiles-of-the-Jewish-People.htm.
84. Ibid.
85. Ibid.
86. Yosef Eisen, "Burning the Talmud," Chabad.org, accessed September 28, 2025, https://www.chabad.org/library/article_cdo/aid/2617032/jewish/Burning-the-Talmud.htm.
87. "Jews in England 1290," The National Archives, accessed September 28, 2025, https://www.nationalarchives.gov.uk/education/resources/jews-in-england-1290/.
88. "Bogdan Chmielnicki," Jewish Virtual Library, accessed September 28, 2025, https://www.jewishvirtuallibrary.org/chmielnicki-khmelnitski-bogdan-x00b0.
89. Rabbi Dovie Schochet, "Discover the Four Exiles of the Jewish People," Chabad.org, https://www.chabad.org/library/article_cdo/aid/3671017/jewish/Discover-the-Four-Exiles-of-the-Jewish-People.htm.
90. "When Did Jews Become White?" *Jewish Currents*, accessed December 1, 2024, https://jewishcurrents.org/when-did-jews-become-white.
91. "Are Jews White?" *Unpacked*, accessed December 1, 2024, https://unpacked.media/are-jews-white.

92. Bruce Goldman, "New Genetic Study: More Evidence for Modern Ashkenazi Jews' Ancient Hebrew Patrimony," Stanford Medicine, December 20, 2013, https://scopeblog.stanford.edu/2013/12/20/new-genetic-study-more-evidence-for-modern-ashkenazi-jews-ancient-hebrew-patrimony.
93. "Statistical Abstract of Israel 2024," Israel Central Bureau of Statistics, last modified May 2024, https://www.cbs.gov.il/he/mediarelease/doclib/2024/141/11_24_141e.pdf.
94. "Ashkenazi Jews Are Not White: Response to Haaretz Article," *The Times of Israel*, accessed December 1, 2024.
95. Jewish Virtual Library, "Vital Statistics: Jewish Population of the World," accessed March 17, 2025, https://www.jewishvirtuallibrary.org/jewish-population-of-the-world.
96. Regena Thomashauer, *Pussy: A Reclamation* (St. Martin's Press, 2019).
97. Pamela Paresky, "Critical Race Theory and the 'Hyper-'White Jew," *Sapir*, Spring 2021, https://sapirjournal.org/social-justice/2021/05/critical-race-theory-and-the-hyper-white-jew/.
98. Kimberlé Crenshaw, "Demarginalizing the Intersection of Race and Sex: A Black Feminist Critique of Antidiscrimination Doctrine, Feminist Theory and Antiracist Politics," University of Chicago Legal Forum 1989, no. 1: 8, http://chicagounbound.uchicago.edu/uclf/vol1989/iss1/8.
99. Lenore J. Weitzman, "Kashariyot (Couriers) in Jewish Resistance During the Holocaust," *The Shalvi/Hyman Encyclopedia of Jewish Women*," accessed March 17, 2025, https://jwa.org/encyclopedia/article/kashariyot-couriers-in-jewish-resistance-during-holocaust.
100. Dr. Rinat Harash, "The 'Humanitarian Doctor' the Media Platformed Was a Hamas Colonel," HonestReporting, February 1, 2026, https://honestreporting.com/the-humanitarian-doctor-the-media-platformed-was-a-hamas-colonel/.
101. Shiryn Ghermezian, "Gaza-Based Journalist Tied to PFLP Terrorist Group Wins Emmy Award for Coverage of Israel-Hamas War," *The Algemeiner*, September 27, 2024, https://www.algemeiner.com/2024/09/27/gaza-based-journalist-tied-to-pflp-terrorist-group-wins-emmy-award-for-coverage-of-israel-hamas-war/.

102. "What Is the PFLP?" NGO Monitor, accessed December 1, 2024, https://ngo-monitor.org/key-issues/ngo-links-to-terror-groups/what-is-the-pflp.
103. "Israel Defense Forces: Ruach Tzahal—Code of Ethics," Jewish Virtual Library, accessed March 29, 2025, https://www.jewishvirtuallibrary.org/ruach-tzahal-idf-code-of-ethics.
104. "Our Mission, Our Values," Israel Defense Forces, accessed March 29, 2025, https://www.idf.il/en/mini-sites/our-mission-our-values/.
105. "Health Misinformation," United States Department of Health and Human Services, last modified September 2022, https://www.hhs.gov/surgeongeneral/reports-and-publications/health-misinformation/index.html#:~:text=Defining%20misinformation,available%20evidence%20at%20the%20time.
106. "Disinformation," National Institute of Standards and Technology, accessed March 29, 2025, https://csrc.nist.gov/glossary/term/disinformation.
107. "Tactics of Disinformation," Cybersecurity and Infrastructure Security Agency (CISA), accessed December 1, 2024, https://www.cisa.gov/sites/default/files/publications/tactics-of-disinformation_508.pdf.
108. Cecilie S. Traberg, Jon Roozenbeek, and Sander van der Linden, "Psychological Inoculation Against Misinformation: Current Evidence and Future Directions," *The ANNALS of the American Academy of Political and Social Science* 700, no. 1 (2022): 116–33, https://doi.org/10.1177/00027162221087936.
109. Sander van der Linden, *Foolproof: Why Misinformation Infects Our Minds and How to Build Immunity* (HarperCollins, 2023).
110. Soroush Vosoughi, Deb Roy, and Sinan Aral, "The Spread of True and False News Online," *Science* 359, no. 6380 (2018): 1146–51, https://doi.org/10.1126/science.aap9559.
111. S. Lewandowsky et al., "Misinformation and Its Correction: Continued Influence and Successful Debiasing," *Psychological Science in the Public Interest* 13, no. 3: 106–31.
112. U. K. H. Ecker et al., "The Psychological Rivers of Misinformation Belief and Its Resistance to Correction," *Nature Reviews Psychology* 1 (2022): 13–29, https://www.nature.com/articles/s44159-021-00006-y.

113. "When Terrorism Is Disguised as Journalism," HonestReporting, January 21, 2025, https://honestreporting.com/when-terrorism-is-disguised-as-journalism/.
114. "Press Release: Major Increase in Online Antisemitism in First Year After October 7 Hamas Attack," CyberWell, October 21, 2024, https://cyberwell.org/post/press-release-major-increase-in-online-antisemitism-in-first-year-after-october-7-hamas-attack/.
115. "The Rapid Spread of Misinformation Following the Israel-Gaza War," Digital Forensic Research Lab, https://www.atlanticcouncil.org/programs/digital-forensic-research-lab.
116. "Did Media Coverage of the Israel-Hamas War Influence the Rise in Post-October 7 Antisemitism?" HonestReporting, accessed December 1, 2024, https://honestreporting.com/did-media-coverage-of-the-israel-hamas-war-influence-the-rise-in-post-october-7-antisemitism/.
117. Josh Levs, "The Mainstream Media Is Biased Against Israel. I Know, I Was Part of It," *Newsweek*, May 7, 2024, https://www.newsweek.com/mainstream-media-biased-against-israel-i-know-i-was-part-it-opinion-1898058.
118. Matti Friedman, "An Insider's Guide to the Most Important Story on Earth," *Tablet*, accessed December 1, 2024.
119. "Bots and Inauthentic Coordinated Propaganda Networks Extensively Targets Celebrities and Influencers Online Amidst Ongoing War," Network Contagion Research Institute, October 18, 2023, https://networkcontagion.us/reports/11-2-23-bots-and-inauthentic-coordinated-propaganda-networks-extensively-targets-celebrities-and-influencers-online-amidst-ongoing-war/.
120. Ibid.
121. C. Martel, G. Pennycook, and D. G. Rand, "Reliance on Emotion Promotes Belief in Fake News," *Cognitive Research: Principles and Implications* 5 (2020): 47, https://doi.org/10.1186/s41235-020-00252-3.
122. "Illusory Truth Effect," The Decision Lab, accessed March 29, 2025, https://thedecisionlab.com/biases/illusory-truth-effect.

123. Aumyo Hassan and Sarah J. Barber, "The Effects of Repetition Frequency on the Illusory Truth Effect," *Cognitive Research: Principles and Implications* 6 (2021): 38, https://doi.org/10.1186/s41235-021-00301-5.

124. Stephan Lewandowsky and Sander van der Linden, "Countering Misinformation and Fake News Through Inoculation and Prebunking," *European Review of Social Psychology* 32, no. 2: 348–84, https://doi.org/10.1080/10463283.2021.1876983.

125. Jonathan Sacks, "The Meanings of Shema," Covenant & Conversation: Va'etchanan, Rabbi Sacks Legacy, accessed March 29, 2025, https://rabbisacks.org/covenant-conversation/vaetchanan/the-meanings-of-shema/.

126. "On Leadership: To Lead Is to Listen," Aish.com, https://aish.com/on-leadership-to-lead-is-to-listen/.

127. Abigail Klein Leichman, "Israeli Agricultural Innovations Will Keep the World Fed," ISRAEL21c, April 24, 2022, updated November 28, 2022, https://www.israel21c.org/israeli-agricultural-innovations-will-keep-the-world-fed/.

128. Corin Degani, "As the World Struggles to Prepare for Water Shortages, Israel Is Sitting Pretty," *Haaretz*, August 14, 2023, https://www.haaretz.com/life/nature-environment/2023-08-14/ty-article-magazine/.premium/as-the-world-struggles-to-prepare-for-water-shortages-israel-is-sitting-pretty/00000189-f3f1-d975-a9cf-fbf3eb930000.

129. Max Kaplan-Zantopp, "How Israel Used Innovation to Beat Its Water Crisis," ISRAEL21c, April 28, 2022, updated February 28, 2023, https://www.israel21c.org/how-israel-used-innovation-to-beat-its-water-crisis/.

130. Shoshana Lichter, "Just as My Ancestors Planted for Me," Jewish National Fund, last modified October 19, 2022, https://www.jnf.org/menu-3/news-media/jnf-wire/jnf-wire-stories/just-as-my-ancestors-planted-for-me.

131. "Our History," Jewish National Fund, accessed March 27, 2025, https://www.jnf.org/our-history.

132. "About Us," TOM Global, accessed March 29, 2025, https://tomglobal.org/about.
133. "Covenant & Conversation: To Lead Is to Listen," Eikev, Rabbi Sacks Legacy, accessed March 29, 2025, https://rabbisacks.org/covenant-conversation/eikev/to-lead-is-to-listen/.
134. "To Paint Is to Live" Holocaust Museum LA, "Art & Resistance in Theresienstadt," accessed December 1, 2024, https://www.holocaustmuseumla.org/topaint.
135. "The Nazi Genocide and Other Persecutions," International Committee of the Red Cross, last modified October 25, 2007, https://www.icrc.org/en/document/wwii-nazi-genocide-and-other-persecutions.
136. "The Red Cross Has Abandoned Israeli Hostages, Middle East Forum," October 2023, https://www.meforum.org/the-red-cross-has-abandoned-israeli-hostages.
137. United States Holocaust Memorial Museum, "Children During the Holocaust," *Holocaust Encyclopedia*, accessed February 13, 2026, https://encyclopedia.ushmm.org/content/en/article/children-during-the-holocaust.
138. Holocaust Museum LA Facts for Kids, *Kiddle Encyclopedia*, accessed February 13, 2026, https://kids.kiddle.co/Holocaust_Museum_LA.
139. "StandWithUs Horrified by Pogrom Attack in Amsterdam," StandWithUs," October 2023, https://www.standwithus.com/post/standwithus-horrified-by-pogrom-attack-in-amsterdam.
140. United States Holocaust Memorial Museum, "Pogroms," *Holocaust Encyclopedia*, accessed December 1, 2024, https://encyclopedia.ushmm.org/content/en/article/pogroms.
141. United States Holocaust Memorial Museum, "Kristallnacht," *Holocaust Encyclopedia*, accessed December 1, 2024, https://encyclopedia.ushmm.org/content/en/article/kristallnacht.
142. "Dutch Police Allowed Officers to Refuse to Protect Jews 1 Month Before Pogrom," Israel National News, November 8, 2024, https://www.israelnationalnews.com/news/398843.
143. Simone Rodan-Benzaquen, "Following the Pogrom in Amsterdam, Europe Must Act Now to Protect Jews," *The Algemeiner*, December 4,

2024, https://www.algemeiner.com/2024/12/04/following-the-pogrom-in-amsterdam-europe-must-act-now-to-protect-jews/.

144. Neil Baldwin, *Henry Ford and the Jews: The Mass Production of Hate* (PublicAffairs, 2001).

145. David K. Smith, "Ford and the Nazis," *The Guardian*, 1999, https://www.theguardian.com/world/1999/aug/20/julianborger1.

146. U.S. Holocaust Memorial Museum, "Collaborators: American Corporations and Nazi Germany."

147. Ibid.

148. "From Dearborn to NYC, Quds Day Protesters Praise Terrorists, Denounce the U.S. and Call for the Destruction of Israel," Anti-Defamation League, April 10, 2024, https://www.adl.org/resources/article/dearborn-nyc-quds-day-protesters-praise-terrorists-denounce-us-and-call.

149. Ibid.

150. David Adesnik and Ahmad Sharawi, "Don't Buy Rashida Tlaib & Co.'s Lie: 'From the River to the Sea' Has Always Meant Erasing Israel," Foundation for Defense of Democracies, May 16, 2024, https://www.fdd.org/analysis/2024/05/16/dont-buy-rashida-tlaib-co-s-lie-from-the-river-to-the-sea-has-always-meant-erasing-israel/.

151. American Jewish Committee, "From the River to the Sea," Translate Hate (American Jewish Committee), accessed February 14, 2026, https://www.ajc.org/translatehate/From-the-River-to-the-Sea.

152. Aish.com, "Why the 'From the River to the Sea' Chant Is Antisemitic," accessed February 14, 2026, https://aish.com/why-the-from-the-river-to-sea-chant-is-antisemitic/.

153. Natan Sharansky, *Fear No Evil* (PublicAffairs, 1998).

154. "Natan Sharansky," *Jewish Virtual Library*, accessed September 28, 2025, https://jewishvirtuallibrary.org/biographies-wing/all-biographies-by-last-name/s/natan-anatoly-sharansky.

155. David Edmonds, "Natan Sharansky: How Chess Kept One Man Sane," BBC News Magazine, January 3, 2014, https://www.bbc.com/news/magazine-25560162.

156. Natan Sharansky, "3D Test of Antisemitism: Demonization, Double Standards, Delegitimization," Jewish Political Studies Review 16, nos.

3–4 (Fall 2004), Jerusalem Center for Public Affairs, https://jcpa.org/article/the-3-d-test-of-antisemitism-demonization-double-standards-delegitimization/.

157. S. Harsey and J. J. Freyd, "Deny, Attack, and Reverse Victim and Offender (DARVO): What Is the Influence on Perceived Perpetrator and Victim Credibility?" *Journal of Aggression, Maltreatment, & Trauma*, 29, no. 8: 897–916, https://doi.org/10.1080/10926771.2020.1774695.

158. Alexander H. Joffe, "Why the Origins of the BDS Movement Matter," Middle East Forum, August 31, 2016, https://www.meforum.org/bds-origins.

159. Aftyn Behn, "Nashville's Nazi Problem," The Behn Factor, Substack, September 28, 2025, https://aftynbehnfortn.substack.com/p/nashvilles-nazi-problem.

160. Joel Fishman, "The Red-Green Alliance and the War against American Jewry, the American-Israel Alliance, and the Foundations of American Democracy," *Jewish Political Studies Review* 30, no. 3/4 (2019): 5–17, Jerusalem Center for Public Affairs.

161. Eran Shayshon, "The Red-Green Alliance Is Coming to America," *Jewish Journal*, December 22, 2021, https://jewishjournal.com/commentary/opinion/343507/the-red-green-alliance-is-coming-to-america/.

162. Michael Starr, "Tucker Carlson at Charlie Kirk Memorial: Like Jesus, Murdered by Guys 'Eating Hummus' in Jerusalem," *The Jerusalem Post*, September 22, 2025, https://www.jpost.com/diaspora/antisemitism/article-868381.

163. "Working Definition of Antisemitism," International Holocaust Remembrance Alliance, accessed March 29, 2025, https://holocaustremembrance.com/resources/working-definition-antisemitism.

164. Ibid.

165. Zulfat Suara, "Bio," Zulfat Suara for Council, accessed February 14, 2026, https://zulfatsuara.com/bio/.

166. Council on American-Islamic Relations, "CAIR Welcomes Tennessee University's Decision to Drop 'Anti-Muslim Summit,'" press release, accessed February 14, 2026, https://www.cair.com/press_releases/cair-welcomes-tennessee-universitys-decision-to-drop-anti-muslim-summit/.
167. "Council on American-Islamic Relations," Canary Mission, accessed March 28, 2025, https://canarymission.org/organization/Council_On_American_Islamic_Relations.
168. Omar Barghouti, "BDS and the Jewish State," *New Republic*, 2019.
169. "About BDS (Boycotts, Divestment, and Sanctions)," NGO Monitor, accessed March 29, 2025, https://ngo-monitor.org/key-issues/bds/about/.
170. Jed Babbin with Herbert London, *The BDS War Against Israel: The Orwellian Campaign to Destroy Israel Through the Boycott, Divestment and Sanctions Movement* (London Center for Policy Research, 2014).
171. Alan M. Dershowitz, *Defending Israel: The Story of My Relationship with My Most Challenging Client* (All Points Books, 2019).
172. "Boycott, Divestment, and Sanctions Campaign (BDS)," Anti-Defamation League, May 24, 2022, https://www.adl.org/resources/backgrounder/boycott-divestment-and-sanctions-campaign-bds.
173. "Tough Questions on the Anti-Israel BDS Movement Answered," American Jewish Committee, January 25, 2023, https://www.ajc.org/news/tough-questions-on-the-anti-israel-bds-movement-answered.
174. The Editors of Encyclopaedia Britannica, "Six-Day War," *Encyclopaedia Britannica*, last updated February 7, 2025, https://www.britannica.com/event/Six-Day-War.
175. Ibid.
176. "Israel Completes Gaza Disengagement," BBC News, 2005.
177. Zolan Kanno-Youngs, "Egypt Builds Wall and Buffer Zone on Gaza Border Amid Rising Tensions," CNN, February 16, 2024, http://www.cnn.com/2024/02/16/middleeast/egypt-wall-buffer-zone-gaza-border-intl-hnk/index.html.

178. "Palestinian Authority Payments to Terrorists," Palestinian Media Watch, 2023.
179. Nahal Toosi, "US Says Palestinians Are Close to Changing 'Pay-for-Slay' program," *Politico*, March 29, 2024, https://www.politico.com/news/2024/03/29/us-says-palestinians-are-close-to-changing-pay-for-slay-program-00149734.
180. Gadi Taub, "How Much Is a Dead Jew Worth?" *Tablet*, February 26, 2025, https://www.tabletmag.com/sections/israel-middle-east/articles/how-much-is-dead-jew-worth.
181. Gideon Sa'ar, caption to Instagram post quoting Palestinian Authority payments to terrorists and their families, Instagram, accessed January 2026, https://www.instagram.com/p/DRPPcCQjDbI/.
182. "Palestinian Attacker Gets Life in Prison for Stabbing Holocaust Survivor to Death," *Times of Israel*, January 4, 2026, https://www.timesofisrael.com/liveblog_entry/palestinian-attacker-gets-life-in-prison-for-stabbing-holocaust-survivor-to-death/.
183. John Spencer, "Palestinian Authority's Terror Payments to Holocaust Survivor," *USA Today*, January 10, 2025, https://www.usatoday.com/story/opinion/2025/01/10/palestinian-authority-terror-payments-holocaust-survivor-israel/77543726007/.
184. San Remo Conference, 1920.
185. "Hamas's Priorities: Propaganda and Terrorism Over Governance," MEMRI, 2023.
186. Glenn Kessler, "What Happened to the 2008 Israeli-Palestinian Peace Talks?" *The Washington Post*, 2009.
187. "The Knesset," Knesset, accessed March 29, 2025, https://www.knesset.gov.il/.
188. Times of Israel Staff, "Obituary: Salim Joubran, First Arab Israeli Supreme Court Justice, Dies at 76," *The Times of Israel*, March 15, 2024, https://www.timesofisrael.com/salim-joubran-first-arab-israeli-supreme-court-justice-dies-at-76/.
189. JNS Staff, "Israeli Population Tops 10 Million for First Time," JNS.org, January 3, 2025, https://www.jns.org/israeli-population-tops-10-million-for-first-time/.

190. "Arab Society in Israel: Challenges and Progress," Israel Democracy Institute, 2021.
191. JNS Staff, "Israeli Population Tops 10 Million for First Time," JNS.org, January 3, 2025, https://www.jns.org/israeli-population-tops-10-million-for-first-time/.
192. "Arab Israelis in Higher Education: Trends, Challenges, and Policy Recommendations," Taub Center for Social Policy Studies in Israel, December 2020, https://www.taubcenter.org.il/wp-content/uploads/2020/12/arabisraelisinhighereducation.pdf.
193. "Arab Citizens in Israel," Israel Ministry of Foreign Affairs, 2023.
194. "Statistical Report on Arab Society in Israel 2021," Israel Democracy Institute, 2021.
195. "Linguistic Diversity in Israel," UNESCO, 2020.
196. "Equality in Israel's Legal Framework," Adalah: The Legal Center for Arab Minority Rights in Israel, 2022.
197. "Top IDF Female Muslim Officer 'Captain Ella' Named as Next Arabic Spokesperson," Haaretz (Israel News: Israel Security), February 3, 2026, https://www.haaretz.com/israel-news/israel-security/2026-02-03/ty-article/.premium/top-idf-female-muslim-officer-captain-ella-named-as-next-arabic-spokesperson/0000019c-24c8-d17f-a3df-fffecbe10000.
198. Benny Morris, *1948: A History of the First Arab-Israeli War* (Yale University Press, 2009).
199. "The United Nations Relief and Works Agency," UNRWA Statistics, 2022.
200. Anita Shapira, *Israel: A History* (Brandeis University Press, 2012).
201. Ilan Pappe, *The Iron Cage: The Story of the Palestinian Struggle for Statehood* (Oxford University Press, 2006).
202. "The 'Apartheid' Nonsense," Jerusalem Institute of Justice, last modified June 11, 2018, https://jij.org/news/the-apartheid-nonsense/.
203. "Mandate for Palestine," League of Nations, 1922.
204. Kirsten Lesage, Kelsey Jo Starr, and William Miner, "Religious Switching into and out of Judaism," Pew Research Center, March 26, 2025.

205. United Nations General Assembly, Convention on the Prevention and Punishment of the Crime of Genocide, December 9, 1948, 78 U.N.T.S. 277, art. II.

206. John Spencer, "The 'Genocide' Slur Against Israel Is an Assault on the U.S. Military," *Tablet*, accessed February 13, 2026, https://www.tabletmag.com/sections/israel-middle-east/articles/genocide-slur-israel-us-military.

207. Reuters, "Israeli Military Says Gaza Polio Vaccination Campaign Completed," Reuters, November 6, 2024, https://www.reuters.com/world/middle-east/israeli-military-says-gaza-polio-vaccination-campaign-completed-2024-11-06/.

208. United Nations General Assembly, Convention on the Prevention and Punishment of the Crime of Genocide, December 9, 1948, 78 U.N.T.S. 277, art. II.

209. Israeli government Gaza aid data portal Government of Israel, "Gaza Aid Data," accessed February 13, 2026, https://gaza-aid-data.gov.il/mainhome/.

210. Anti-Defamation League, "The Allegation That Israel Commits Genocide," accessed February 13, 2026, https://www.adl.org/resources/backgrounder/allegation-israel-commits-genocide.

211. Bari Weiss, "A Free Press Conversation with Natan Sharansky," *The Free Press*, November 21, 2024, https://www.thefp.com/p/a-free-press-conversation-with-natan.

212. J. Staff, "U.C. Berkeley Student Senate Passes Resolution Calling for Divestment," *The Jewish News of Northern California*, April 19, 2013, https://jweekly.com/2013/04/19/divestment-back-in-front-of-cal-student-senate/.

213. Rich Calder, "Antisemitic Activist Pushing Zohran Mamdani's NYC Mayoral Bid," *New York Post*, March 22, 2025, https://nypost.com/2025/03/22/us-news/antisemitic-activist-pushing-zohran-mamdanis-nyc-mayoral-bid/.

214. "Columbia Intifada, Canary Mission," accessed December 1, 2024.

215. Chris Nesi, "Families of Hamas Hostages Claim Anti-Israel Protest Groups, Like Columbia's Students for Justice in Palestine Had

'Prior Knowledge' of Oct. 7 Attack in Bombshell Suit," *New York Post*, March 25, 2025. https://nypost.com/2025/03/25/us-news/families-of-hamas-hostages-claim-anti-israel-protest-groups-like-columbias-students-for-justice-in-palestine-had-prior-knowledge-of-oct-7-attack-in-bombshell-suit/.

216. "From Tehran to Columbia: Inside America's Student Intifada," Canary Mission, January 30, 2025, https://canarymission.org/campaign/Columbia_Intifada.
217. Shabbos Kestenbaum, X, March 14, 2025.
218. Julian J. Giordano, Caroline G. Hennigan, and Bradford D. Kimball, "Harvard Law School Students Pass Referendum Urging University to Divest from Israel," *The Harvard Crimson*, March 14, 2025, https://www.thecrimson.com/article/2025/3/14/hls-divestment-referendum-passes/.
219. Julian J. Giordano, Caroline G. Hennigan, and Bradford D. Kimball, "Harvard Law School Students Pass Referendum Urging University to Divest from Israel," *The Harvard Crimson*, March 14, 2025, https://www.thecrimson.com/article/2025/3/14/hls-divestment-referendum-passes/.
220. Ewan Somerville, "Half of British Publishers 'Won't Take Books by Jewish Authors,'" *The Telegraph*, March 3, 2024, http://www.telegraph.co.uk/news/2024/03/03/half-of-british-publishers-wont-take-jewish-authors.
221. Philissa Cramer, "Is Your Fav Author a Zionist? A Viral List Reignites Antisemitism Fears in the Literary World," Jewish Telegraphic Agency, May 9, 2024, https://www.jta.org/2024/05/09/israel/is-your-fav-author-a-zionist-a-viral-list-reignites-antisemitism-fears-in-the-literary-world.
222. "FAQs on the Boston Mapping Project," Anti-Defamation League, accessed March 29, 2025, https://www.adl.org/boston-mapping-project.
223. "5 Reasons Why the BDS Mapping Project Is Dangerous for Jews (and Everyone Else)," American Jewish Committee, June 21, 2022, https://www.ajc.org/news/5-reasons-why-the-bds-mapping-project-is-dangerous-for-jews-and-everyone-else.

224. Michael Starr, "Chicago Bookstore Removes Novel from Book Club Poll Due to 'Zionist' Author, Sparking Controversy," *The Jerusalem Post*, July 23, 2024, https://www.jpost.com/diaspora/antisemitism/article-811560.
225. Nadia Khomami, "Nobel and Pulitzer Winners Denounce 'Dangerous' Israel Cultural Boycott," *The Guardian*, October 30, 2024, https://www.theguardian.com/world/2024/oct/30/nobel-and-pulitzer-winners-denounce-israel-cultural-boycott.
226. Riham Alkousaa and Layli Foroudi, "Palestinian Keffiyeh Scarves: A Controversial Symbol of Solidarity," Reuters, December 15, 2023, https://www.reuters.com/world/middle-east/palestinian-keffiyeh-scarves-controversial-symbol-solidarity-2023-12-14/.
227. David Propper and Alex Oliveira, "BLM Chicago Under Fire for Pro-Palestine Post Featuring Paragliding Terrorist: 'Disgusting and Disgraceful,'" *New York Post*, October 10, 2023, https://nypost.com/2023/10/10/blm-chicago-under-fire-for-pro-palestine-post-featuring-paragliding-terrorist/.
228. "Congressional Testimony Highlights Ties Between Hamas-Linked Charities and BDS," *The Times of Israel*, accessed March 29, 2025, http://www.timesofisrael.com/congressional-testimony-highlights-ties-between-hamas-linked-charities-bds.
229. "Campus BDS Backgrounder," American Jewish Committee, accessed May 27, 2025, https://www.ajc.org/campusbds.
230. "Behind the Boycott: The History of the Hateful Campaign Against Israel" American Jewish Committee, accessed May 27, 2025, https://www.ajc.org/behindtheboycott.
231. "What Is BDS?" StandWithUs, accessed May 27, 2025, https://www.standwithus.com/factsheets-bds.
232. "About NGO Monitor," NGO Monitor, accessed May 27, 2025, https://www.ngo-monitor.org/about/.
233. "Jewish Voice for Peace: Whitewashing Antisemitism in the Anti-Israel Movement," HonestReporting, accessed May 27, 2025, https://honestreporting.com/jewish-voice-for-peace-whitewashing-antisemitism-in-the-anti-israel-movement/.

234. Ron Kampeas, "ADL Announces Opposition to Israel's Anti-BDS Law," *Forward*, March 8, 2017, https://forward.com/news/breaking-news/365434/adl-is-second-establishment-jewish-group-to-oppose-israel-s-anti-bds-law/.
235. "Key Findings About Americans' Declining Trust in Government and Each Other," Pew Research Center, accessed December 1, 2024, https://www.pewresearch.org/politics/2019/07/22/trust-and-distrust-in-america/.
236. "Views of the State of Moral Values in the U.S. Hit a New Low," Gallup, accessed December 1, 2024, https://news.gallup.com/poll/506960/views-state-moral-values-new-low.aspx.
237. "Surgeon General Social Connection Advisory," United States Department of Health and Human Services, accessed December 1, 2024, https://www.hhs.gov/sites/default/files/surgeon-general-social-connection-advisory-pdf.
238. United States Holocaust Memorial Museum, "The Weimar Republic," *Holocaust Encyclopedia*, accessed March 23, 2025, https://encyclopedia.ushmm.org/content/en/article/the-weimar-republic.
239. Raphael Shore, "Who's Afraid of the Big Bad Jew?" October 2024.
240. Wolfgang G. Schwanitz, "Photographic Evidence Shows Palestinian Leader Amin al-Husseini at a Nazi Concentration Camp," *Tablet*, April 7, 2021, https://www.tabletmag.com/sections/news/articles/amin-al-husseini-nazi-concentration-camp.
241. U.S. Holocaust Memorial Museum, "Hajj Amin al-Husseini: Wartime Propagandist," accessed December 1, 2024, https://encyclopedia.ushmm.org/content/en/article/hajj,amin,al,husayni,wartime,propagandist.

INDEX

ABOUT THE AUTHOR

Alyssa Rosenheck is a bestselling author, advocate, and one of *Architectural Digest*'s Top 50 Interior and Architectural Photographers in the United States. Her debut book, *The New Southern Style* (Abrams), reframed creativity as a vehicle for resilience, courage, and connection—revealing how art has the power to humanize our differences and remind us of our shared humanity.

Beyond her creative career, Alyssa is a leading voice in the fight against antisemitism and a fearless advocate for Israel. She was honored with the 2025 *Hero Against Hate* award by the ADL and is a founding member of Artists Against Antisemitism. Since October 7th, she has traveled to Israel multiple times as a post-war delegate, participated in the UN Global Summit with the AJC, and collaborates closely with organizations including the AJC, ADL, StandWithUs, Consulate General of Israel to the South Eastern United States, and CUFI. Her grassroots impact is wide-ranging: she has mobilized communities alongside state legislators, played a key role in stopping two BDS resolutions at the city council level, and is actively engaged with the Tennessee-Israel Caucus. She regularly publishes op-eds challenging BDS, anti-American, and antisemitic ideologies, and speaks on college campuses to educate and equip the next generation to stand for truth and defend democratic values.

Additionally, Alyssa confronts the modern challenges of social media, using her platform to expose propaganda, counter extremism, and amplify civic responsibility. Alyssa's work is a testament to the belief that creativity is not just a personal pursuit—it is a collective responsibility for truth-tellers, a tool for moral courage, and a force for building stronger bridges.